Learning to Live Again

Learning to Live Again

by

Susan Lesley

DORRANCE PUBLISHING CO., INC.
PITTSBURGH, PENNSYLVANIA 15222

ISBN: 978-0-8059-7595-6
Library of Congress Control Number: 2006940742

Printed in the United States of America

First Printing

For more information or to order additional books, please contact:
Dorrance Publishing Co., Inc.
701 Smithfield Street
Third Floor
Pittsburgh, Pennsylvania 15222
U.S.A.
1-800-788-7654
www.dorrancebookstore.com

This book is dedicated to all the men, women, and children who have survived any form of abuse. It is said what does not kill you, can only make you stronger; therefore, this is a testimony of my strength and courage in hopes that it will touch the many out there who are still suffering the bondage of verbal, physical, sexual, or emotional abuse.

I never thought in my wildest dreams that I would be a success in any way, shape, or form. It was just a few years ago that I wanted to end my life. My spirit had been broken, and I felt like I had no soul. Nothing but the love of my children kept me going, for I knew that, without me, they would have no one. For all practical purposes, I was dead inside. This was due to five long years of the constant belittling and torment I endured from my now ex-husband. I am not sure when all this self doubt and lack of self-esteem originated, but after stepping back and taking a long, hard look back into the beginning of my childhood, I would have to say it began a long time ago. We all have this concept of ourselves and make strong statements about what we will and what we will not do in certain situations. Somewhere along the way, things change and we become people we never thought we would be. So where did it all begin for me, and how did life become so incredibly cruel that I would even consider doing the unthinkable?

I was the youngest of four children, born in Minneapolis, Minnesota in 1958, living in a suburban neighborhood where the term "dysfunctional families" only existed among the poor and unspoken. My family was all but functional. All I am able to remember of life is a father, whom I feared with a raging temper and who used the belt to express his rage, and a mother, who screamed constantly. My mother, a gentle soul by nature, was always running interference between my father and us kids. Many times, she would yell for my father to stop hitting us when he appeared out of control. In those days, whatever the man of the house felt was an appropriate punishment was what the wife had to accept, but my mother always made her children a first priority and would only allow my dad so much abusive freedom. My older sister and brother were my comfort since I was the baby, and, yes, there was a fourth child, the oldest sister, who was fifteen years my elder. She was never around much; she was the apple of my father's eye. She was the beauty with the brains, and my father would always say, "Why can't you kids be more like your oldest sister?" I never really got to know my oldest sister, but I do remember being a flower girl at her wedding, walking down the isle of the synagogue as she took her vows. It was a happy day, even if I didn't know her very well. I never understood why she felt so much animosity towards me. Later, I realized that the fact that I was the baby and, in her mind, was a spoiled brat was enough to warrant these feelings. As a child, I was quite hurt by her actions and her tone towards me, but, as time went by, I became numb to her demeanor, and I came to realize it was not my fault how she felt. My other sister, who is four years older than me, was my father's whipping post. A wrong look from her in my father's direction gave her quite a few beatings. She could never do anything right according to him and was the brunt of his anger on many occasions. As for my brother, well, being the only boy was his saving grace, so he could do no wrong. I just hid behind my mother as much as possible when the yelling or the hitting began. My brother would later become the only real male role model I would ever have in my life, and he is my best friend, a father figure, if you will. As a child, I was afraid of everything: the dark, rain and thunder, loud voices, and scary movies. I would wet my bed frequently, and Mother would try hard to hide it from my dad because that would mean a spanking if he knew. So there were many nights I would lay in urine until morning, then tell my mom. On the nights when I woke my dad and I did receive a spanking or the belt, my mother would rub lotion on my blistered bottom after he was done as I lay and cried for hours. Sometimes I would crawl in bed with my parents if the fear was too much to bear, and, being the baby, this was allowed. I felt safe lying between my mom and dad, and despite everything, I felt loved feeling the warmth of their bodies next to mine. I had no idea at that time my father was a womanizer, a pill popper, and he loved his booze. I had lost my grandfathers before I was even born, and my grandmothers were quite old and not the typical spoiling, loving people that grandmothers are supposed to be. My father would come home late at night and be drunk and disruptive, and my mother would just tell us kids to go back to bed and be quiet.

The winters in Minnesota were so cold and bitter. We would go sledding down our driveway and make angels in the snow. The house we lived in looked so big to me as a child, but years later, when I returned to Minnesota for my father's funeral and saw that house again, it was tiny, and the driveway that seemed so steep, where I rode my bike down and skinned my knee was nothing like I had remembered. I had this little playmate in nursery school named Eddie. He and I would spend hours playing. One day my babysitter found Eddie and I under the covers fondling each other, you know, our private parts. She told us that it was dirty and we could hurt each other doing such a thing. All I knew was that it felt good, and I could not conceive of anything that felt that good possibly being so wrong. It was my first sexual encounter as a child.

My father and mother had another couple that they were very close to, and since my father was such a poor excuse for a husband, my mother found herself finding comfort in the arms of this other man, who was also in a loveless marriage. In those days, divorce was taboo, and you stayed together at all costs. My father found out and went after the other man with a gun. Needless to say, no one was hurt, but we did end up moving away when I was entering kindergarten. That other man stayed with his wife and later, to my dismay, would become my stepfather. So off we went in our stationwagon across country to California, to a suburb called Montevello, California. My father had landed a job there, and we bought this big, beautiful four bedroom, two story house. My sister, brother, and myself got to pick out the colors of our rooms and had all new furniture. My room was the smallest, and pink was the color I chose. I don't think I spent more than one complete night in that room because, again, I was always scared of something and ended up in my parents' bed. My father was a salesman of some sort and was gone the majority of the time, which made things around the house quite pleasant. I made a little friend right away whom I will never forget as long as I live. She used to come to school with horrible blisters on the palms of her hands. When I asked how she got so hurt, she told me that her mother would put her hands on the hot stove to punish her. I ran home to tell my mother, and my mother said we needed to mind our own business. I never understood how my mother could look the other way when it came to a child, but in those days everyone did. This little girl will forever be in my thoughts.

Our trip to California was another good memory for me. We sang songs, stopped to see different tourist attractions like the Grand Canyon, and you could say it was a Kodak kind of trip. It would be the last good memory of our family that I would ever have. Soon after the move, my father lost his job, and so we lost the house, and the new furniture went back to the stores from which it came. My oldest sister, who was married with two young boys and lived in Birmingham, Alabama, had suggested we move out there to be with them. So, back in the stationwagon we went and headed south.

It was a very long trip to Alabama with three kids, a dog, and two adults, but we finally made it there, and the real nightmare was about to begin. The apartment we rented was two bedrooms, red brick, and old. It had hardwood floors and old, rusty appliances. It was very crowded, and all of us kids went from having our own rooms to sharing one room. My father took a job at a vending company downtown, which wouldn't last long, and my mother looked after us kids. One afternoon on a weekend, we all went roller skating, and my father fell and broke his leg. That was the end of him working. The vending company took pity on our family and gave my mother a job as a bookkeeper in a rat infested office making a hundred dollars a week at the most, just enough to keep us fed and a roof over our heads. My father sat in his recliner all day drinking beer, eating, and watching television. One day, my mother said she had had enough of this life and asked my father for a divorce. My father tried to overdose on pain pills and ended up in a veterans hospital, where they administered electric shock treatments for a diagnosis of acute depression. This did not stop my mother from going through with the divorce, and my father finally gave in to the inevitable and went back to Minnesota. We were rid of the old ball and chain called Dad.

My life in the south was a child's horror story. I was in second grade at the time, and there I was too tall, too skinny, and had buck teeth from sucking my thumb as a small child. Not to mention, I was Jewish and was from the North. So, to these southern rednecks, I was a dirty Jew and a damn Yankee. There were absolutely no Black, Hispanic, or Oriental people in my school. I had a teacher who hated Jews and Yankees, so every time she saw fit, she would find a reason to hit me across the head or on the hands with a ruler or her hair brush. She would make me get up in front of the class every morning and read out of the bible, and if I cried, she would tell the whole class, "Look at the baby crying," to humiliate me. My mother tried to go to the principal of the school and get me out of that teacher's class, but the principal would not listen to any of it.

She insisted on keeping me in that class. I stayed home more than I was in school that year due to the abuse. Somehow they let me go on to the third grade. The kids were just as cruel. They would ask me where my tail was because there used to be an old fallacy that Jewish people had tails. They knew my last name was Wolf, so they would yell out, "Wolf, Wolf," as I passed them in the hallway or would call me "bucky beaver" because of my teeth. When my grandmother paid for braces, they called me other names like "brace face" or "wirehead," etc., whatever they could think of at the time. This went on daily. It was the first time I encountered bigotry and abuse for who I was and how I looked. There was no escape. I would never be the same again after the years I spent in the South. I did have one friend who was also Jewish, but she was never in my class. She did live in the same apartments. Her parents were survivors of the Holocaust but spoke nothing of that. They just seemed happy to be in the United States. When I wasn't with her, I was alone. I spent hours daydreaming of moving far away from the hell in which I was in. My mind was in a million other places to escape the environment that I had to tolerate. My mother was at work all day and raising three children on her own, so the afternoons were left up us to stay out of trouble and take care of each other. My brother became the neighborhood bully, and my sister, who was now a young teenager, started hanging with the fast crowd. At the ripe old age of seventeen, my sister got pregnant and married a guy much older than herself. My oldest sister and her family, who were the reason we moved out there, found themselves leaving Alabama and going to the big city of Atlanta, Georgia, where my sister worked as a psychologist, and her husband opened several small businesses. We, however, were stuck in Birmingham. Mother worked so hard to support us without any child support from my dad and no other source of income. She always got us what we needed, but for me, the loneliness was unbearable. My love for animals was something

I always had, and I met a girl who had a horse. She let me ride one day, and from then on I begged my mother to buy me a horse. After a year of begging, she had saved enough money and, low and behold, bought me a horse. A little paint gelding that we kept at a stable close by. My mother would take me to ride every weekend. The loneliness was bearable now that I had this friend that would carry me on his back up into the forest and up and down mountains. It was my final escape hatch from the life I hated. This, however, was not to last long. Soon after I got my horse, my mother received a call from a friend of hers in Minnesota. Remember that couple who were friends of my parents? The man with whom my mother got involved. Well, his wife had died, and he was now living in Beverly Hills, California. My mother got his address from a mutual friend and sent him a sympathy card. Not long after that, the phone rang, and guess who? Yep, it was him. Paul was his name. My mother would stay on the phone for hours laughing and acting like a young schoolgirl with a crush. I was so glad to see her so happy for the first time in years. Life had not been good to my mother, and she deserved to find happiness, regardless of what it meant for us kids. I just didn't know what was in store for us from this happy reunion.

Mother was soon wrapped up in this long lost relationship and began meeting Paul in New Orleans, San Francisco and other spots in the U.S. They had those old sparks ignited, and marriage came next. Another life changing experience was about to take place for me and my family. I was too young to really understand these things, and all I knew was that my mother, my only role model and protector, was being taken away by a stranger. Before I knew it, I had to sell my horse and get ready to be carted off to a Jewish overnight camp in North Carolina called Camp Blue Star while my mother and soon-to-be stepfather were to get married and go on their honeymoon. My sister, who was pregnant and married at the age of seventeen, would stay in Alabama. My brother was sent away to a school called Judson in Arizona. I was miserable at the camp. I had braces on my teeth, was tall and skinny and a downright ugly duckling, and was teased unmercifully. I stayed alone most of the time, and my cabinmates found humor in putting toothpaste all over me one night at my expense. This situation could not have gotten worse. I counted the days until I would see my mother again.

I finally got picked up by my oldest sister and her husband from that horrible camp. I would soon be back with my mother and new stepfather in Beverly Hills, California. There was fear and excitement when I got off the plane at the L.A. airport and saw my mother for the first time in several weeks. She looked so beautiful with new clothes and a huge smile on her face. There was a big diamond ring on her left hand and an even bigger sapphire and gold ring on the right hand. There was a gold and diamond watch, which was engraved inside the band, as well as solid gold lighters for both my mother and Paul with their names engraved on the top that flips open to light cigarettes. Both my mother and Paul were heavy smokers. After I got over the shock of seeing my mother transformed, I got the tour of Beverly Hills and ended up in a security apartment complex one block over from Beverly Drive. I could walk to Rodeo Drive and all the shops and restaurants. I could have learned to really enjoy this life, but all that glitters is not gold. We lived on the south side of the tracks, which means that north of Santa Monica Boulevard are the big houses where the movie stars live. South of Santa Monica Boulevard were the smaller homes and apartment complexes where I lived. Our apartment had two bedrooms and was very dark and dreary inside. Everything was very elegant and uncomfortable. It was nothing like I had been used to. What was even worse was that Paul hated kids. It was obvious the day we met. He was a short, stocky man with a round face. His voice was always condescending, and he wanted nothing to do with me or my brother. I again felt so alone. My mother would feed me dinner, and then she would sit down with Paul for their dinner meal together. Never did we have a meal together as a so-called family. I hated this man who was now my stepfather. He stole my mother from me and sent my brother away. We would pass each other in the hall and never say a word to each other. Paul was an abused child himself, and even though he had been married before and had adult children, he never knew how to relate to them. He was brilliant and supported us in a style for which he should be commended, but I was only twelve years old, so his brilliance was not a factor. Working for Columbia studios, he would pull strings, and I would be allowed on the sets of certain shows that were filming. This was his way of trying to bond with me but to no avail. I would never accept this man in my life.

Shortly after I moved to Beverly Hills, my brother was to return home. He got kicked out of Judson private school for smoking marijuana. I was no longer alone. My brother was back, and we had to get a bigger place to live. My mom and stepfather rented a penthouse apartment, still in the Beverly Hills city limits, which was perfect for all of us. There was a separate hallway with two bedrooms and bathrooms, which were for my brother and myself. The rest of the penthouse was our parents'. Our rooms were right next to the front door, so we could go in and out without even being seen. I felt like it was my brother and me against the world.

The days to come were filled with going to school and trying to make friends. I was considered a geek, and no one really was very friendly to me. I was from the South and had a thick Southern accent, which I had to work hard to lose if I wanted to fit in. I was surrounded by rich, snobby kids, and after several weeks of school, I finally met a girl in my grade named Andrea. She would become my best friend for many years to come.

Andrea and I did everything together. On the weekends, she would stay overnight at my house, and we would take the bus to the movies or the beach. My brother made several friends that first year, but he was in the drug crowd. He smoked marijuana and took LSD as well as other drugs that were popular in those days. I was this little prude that made straight A's in school and never got into trouble, but soon that little girl would be a holy terror.

My mother and I started to grow apart, and Andrea and our small circle of friends became my world. On occasion we would end up hanging out with the faster crowd with my brother and his friends. One day while in my room with Andrea, we looked at each other and said let's go ask my brother if he will get us high. Yes, we were ready to take that next step and go to another level of adolescence. So we did, and from then on, life would never be the same. Another life changing event in a crazy kind of way.

No matter where we are in our lives, I have come to realize that we are exactly where we are supposed to be, and life changing experiences come in different forms. It could be a birth, a death, a new job, a new relationship, or a loss of the job or relationship. Whatever the case my be, your life will never be the same, and only upon reflection of such experiences do we realize the gravity of which these experiences changed our lives.

From that day, in my brothers bathroom, when I put a pipe to my mouth and became a user of drugs, I started a series of events that would bring heartache and tragedy. I took everything to the limit. I just wanted to be popular and have fun. I was thirteen and in eighth grade about to enter Beverly Hills High School. Another life changing experience was entering the high school of all the stars' children. Who was I? Just a poor kid from Alabama, and now I really felt inferior. I had no self confidence and thought I was an ugly duckling with this large nose and an awkward figure. Taller than my friends and very shy, I was going to try to make it work in this new environment, but it wasn't meant to be for very long. I soon got involved with a group of kids who were older and guys who had their brains in their pants. It was time to step up to the plate and give up my virginity at the ripe old age of fourteen or be tortured and ridiculed by my so-called friends who had all had that experience. Andrea was also a virgin, so this was going to be a group effort: friends forever and everything together. Plans were made with two boys who were Juniors. My guy's name was Steve, and we were at a friend's house where the parents had gone to Palm Springs for the weekend.

Steve and I were starting to get all hot and heavy, and off came the clothes. I was terrified. His hands traveled down my body, and his lips where all over my mouth and neck. I remember feeling like this whole thing was so wrong. I didn't love this guy, hell I don't even think I knew him well enough to say that I even liked him. I was doing this out of pure peer pressure. His hard penis felt like a drill trying to pry my legs apart. It was hurting so badly that I began to scream, "Stop, stop," but he kept on until I pushed him off me. I couldn't do it. I don't know if it was physically too painful or I freaked out. I had done it this time. This made me look like the idiot of the year. I now had the reputation of being the worst lay Steve ever had, and everyone knew about it. The worst thing was that I was still a virgin. He had never penetrated me, and still I was the worst lay he ever had. I had to fix this, or my life would be a living hell.

I was on a mission now to try and find someone who would make me feel comfortable enough to go through with it. I knew a guy who was just a friend. His name was Jack, and he was older and had been with some of my friends. After talking to him about my dilemma, he was very receptive to the idea of helping me out. What sixteen-year-old male wouldn't be receptive to this offer? Andrea was in love with Jack, and this was the only drawback. I really needed to know that she would understand that this was not going to ruin our friendship. Jack had been her first, so it was kind of another experience we could share. Remember we were only fourteen going on seventeen. Growing up in California was quite a education, as you will see.

Jack and I planned this night together, and it worked out beautifully. He was so sweet and gentle, always asking if I was alright as he caressed my body, and we became one together. It didn't hurt like before. It was as if he knew exactly how to make me feel loved. The night ended with hugs and kisses but only friendship was agreed to. He would be a part of my life again only many years down the road.

The problem was taken care of now, and I had to show the rest of the crowd that I had become one of them. I became easy, promiscuous, a sure thing, whatever you want to call it. I went from one extreme to the other, and my reputation was that of a whore. I felt like my self worth depended on how many guys wanted me. It did not matter why they wanted me, just that they showed me the attention I never got from any male figure in my life. School became a place that only was an irritant to me. I became rebellious and would cut class and hitchhike to the beach with Andrea and spend the day getting high. I was a spoiled child gone wild. I felt free to do whatever the whim would allow. I didn't care about anyone but myself. Doesn't this sound just like a typical teenager?

This went on for the next year when I became involved with the law. There had been an incident where two friends and myself decided to go to the mall by the beach and see how much we could steal. Well, needless to say, we got caught, and our parents had to come get us out of the Santa Monica Jail. Another incident was when I was babysitting for our next door neighbors' son and had a big party where the Beverly Hills police where called and everyone got busted. Never did I see the inside of a court room because my stepfather had plenty of money to bail me out of whatever situation came about. Once I went joy riding with my mother's car, hit a bunch of parked cars, and left the scene of the accident. Later that night, the doorbell rang after Andrea and I had told my mom that someone had hit our car and took off. It was the police standing at our doorway investigating a hit and run to several cars. I got busted for that one, too. No court! Amazing what you can get away with when you live in Beverly Hills and your stepfather is wealthy.

I caused my poor mother more aggravation and put her through so much hell, I seriously cant believe she didn't get rid of me somehow. But she still told me that she loved me no matter what. One day I happened to be home by myself just sitting in my room. My brother was gone with his friends, and my stepfather happened to be in town that weekend. I heard a scream coming from my mother and stepfather's room. My stepfather was lying on the bed very still. His lips were blue, and there was no breaths coming from out of his mouth. My mother was standing over him and picking up the phone to call emergency 911. My stepfather was a pill freak. He had more pills in his medicine cabinet than you would see in a pharmacy, all different colors and all different strengths doing all different kinds of things, from keeping you up to making you sleep, from relaxing your muscles to relieving your pain. He had it all. Now he lay there, lifeless and unable to move. My mother was sobbing over him, and the paramedics were trying to make his heart start beating again. With paddles to his chest and his body bouncing with every electro shock, they got a rhythm. He was then transferred to UCLA Medical center I.C.U., where only my mother was allowed to visit; where she sat by his side every waking hour until the doctors thought he was stable. It was touch and go, but he was starting to come to when I made a visit to see him. They allowed me in his room, and I said it was good to see him awake. He motioned me to lean down, and in a soft whisper he said, "I love you" to me. I began to cry and left the room. This man I hated so much was tying to let me know that he didn't hate me after all. All of a sudden, my mother came running out of the room, and all you could see were staff nurses and doctors run in with equipment in hand. My stepfather was coding, and this time he wouldn't make it. Within minutes of entering the room, the staff came slowly out, and we knew that Paul was gone. His heart had stopped for no real apparent reason. Not seventy-two hours after his arrival to UCLA medical center, my stepfather was dead. This was another life changing experience.

The days and weeks to come were spent with my mother. The funeral was quite the show with several people in the movie industry from Columbia studios and friends Paul had whom I had never met. There were people whom I would never come in contact with again in my life or in my mother's life. These were Paul's friends, and life became very quiet once things settled down. One day, as my mother and I were going through Paul's things, my mother came across a note. It said, "Thoughts of me shall never be forgotten, Love Paul." My mother began to cry. It was apparent that Paul had every intention to end his life, and the note proved that. This had to remind mother of her father's suicide. I never knew my grandfather because he died before I was born. All I knew was that my mother adored her father, and he ended his life in his garage as he let the car run. My grandmother found him, and this was an embarrassment to the family at that time. We always were made to believe that he had died of a heart attack. We later found out the truth.

Paul had left Mother set financially but only if she used the money wisely. That would be the hard part. None of my friends came around for months. They were too immature to call and stated that they just didn't know what to say. You really find out who your friends are when things like this happen. I knew my mother needed me, and I needed her.

As the months passed, and now that Paul was gone, we would have to downsize. I was sixteen and had a car of my own, which Mother bought with the money Paul had left her. She also bought a car for my brother, who graduated from Beverly Hills High School and was starting in college working on a degree in auto mechanics. I was also given a nose job by a famous plastic surgeon on Beverly Drive, for which I had begged my mom for years. Money was being spent quickly, and we found ourselves moving closer to the beach in Brentwood, California near UCLA campus. There were fraternity houses everywhere and parties every weekend. Even though I had moved out of Beverly Hills, all my friends had cars and would drive to the frat parties. Life was full of good times, and things like school took the back burner. I was failing my classes and started studying for my GED. I couldn't hack being in school, and I wasn't smart enough to realize what effect those decisions would have on my future.

One afternoon as I was driving in my neighborhood, I spotted two boys who looked to be in their late teens on skateboards. I stopped the car, introduced myself to them, and told them where I lived. One was short with blonde hair and blue eyes, and his name was Paul. Then there was Richard, who was tall and thin with brown hair and brown eyes. Richard and I were drawn to each other. From the moment we laid eyes on one another, we knew that we were meant to be. I spent every day with him from the time we met. I would sneak him in my room at night, and he would spend the night. I was in love, and for the first time, it was real.

I was going on seventeen, thinking I knew it all, and my mom tried to guide me away from Richard. He had no ambition and was a high school drop-out, not someone of whom my mother approved. During this time, we received a phone call from my oldest sister in Georgia. She was going through a divorce and wanted us to move there. Mother literally had no one after Paul died, and she felt like I was growing up way too fast in California. Besides, in her mind, we had enough money left that if, after six months, we didn't like it there, we could move back. I rejected the idea but lost the battle. We were moving again, and it was back to the South. I knew I would hate it there, and without Richard, I was going to be miserable. We all caravanned in single file across country in separate cars, stopping to rest overnight as we set out for Atlanta, Georgia.

I would still keep in touch with Richard and would be back with him eventually. Once settled in an apartment in a rural area outside of Atlanta called Dunwoody, I found myself in a familiar situation. Everyone I would meet would have some kind of stupid anti-Semitic joke when they found out I was Jewish or would act like we were still fighting the Civil War and call me a damn Yankee. I had stepped back in time, and it reminded me of my younger days in Birmingham, Alabama with all those rednecks. Six months went by, and I got my GED. I started going to a nearby community college and took business courses. I learned how to type and do accounting. My mother always said if you can type, you will never be without a job. I had managed to stay in contact with Richard through all this and made a trip back to L. A. I stayed with Andrea, and when I saw Richard, we were still in love. I wasn't going back to Georgia without him. I was almost eighteen, and this was what we both wanted. My mother wasn't happy, and she made it clear that we couldn't stay with her. I quit college and got a job at a nearby flower shop. Richard got a job doing carpentry, and we quickly got an apartment of our own.

Somehow when you're young and in love, you get caught up in the moment and again don't think things through. We found ourselves in front of a justice of the peace and got married. Just a couple friends were witnesses, but no family. We were so young and living with the bare necessities, with ugly, old furniture, working and getting nowhere. A year later, money was going to drugs, and Richard was spending more time out of work than in work. We fought night and day. The final straw was finding him with a fifteen-year-old runaway in my bed. I sent him back to California and notified him later of the divorce I filed through an add in the paper so he could not contest it. He was angry and hurt, but love just wasn't enough. I knew it was my first real love, and now it was gone.

Living back with my mother was nice and safe. It felt good, and even though I learned a hard lesson with Richard, she loved me unconditionally and welcomed me back with open arms. She was always a gentle soul with a comforting way that made everyone around her feel wanted. She was there for our friends and for a stranger. She always let me keep the stray animals I would bring home and never did she strike me when I didn't deserve it. She had become my best friend through all this, and she knew I needed time to heal. It was shortly after I moved back home that my mother got some shocking news from her last mammogram. The doctors found cancer in my mother's breast, and she had to have surgery. The big "C" had come into our lives, and we were all scared. My brother and two sisters were all around Mom as they rolled her into surgery. It took several hours before the doctor came out and told us that he felt like he had gotten it all but took both breasts and nodes. In other words, my mother had a double radical mastectomy. We were all relieved that she had made it through the surgery but knew it would be a long recovery. Luckily, she did not have to have any chemotherapy or radiation. I was home a lot back then and was able to help mother through the recovery. Money was running out by this time, and we had pretty much resigned ourselves to staying in Georgia. The whole family was here now, and Mother got a job as a bookkeeper at the Jewish community center in downtown Atlanta. I got a job at an advertising agency as an accounts receivable clerk. My brother had graduated with a degree in automotive technology and was scoping out jobs all over the U.S. but finally landed a job with a big dealership close by.

My job at the advertising agency was a lot of fun. The people there consisted of two other women besides myself and two men who actually owned the company. We did a lot of promotional ads for restaurants, bars, rock groups, concert promoters, and radio stations. We always had V.I.P. tickets to events or concerts, and it was a job that was right up my alley being from the west coast, and, well, you know, a little on the wild side. One night, all the girls from the office decided to go out for happy hour at a local steakhouse. We ordered several pitchers of martinis and ended up at one of their houses. It was my one and only bi-sexual experience, and it was between friends. We had to be really drunk, if you know what I mean. The other wild experience with this group of people from the advertising agency was when the owners rented a houseboat for the weekend, and there were about twenty people there, and it lasted day and night. These people were heavy cocaine users, and it was the beginning of a long addiction to cocaine that almost ruined my life. It was a stage of my life when I received the news that my father was found dead in his apartment in Minneapolis, Minnesota. My sisters and brother along with myself flew to Minneapolis for his funeral. We were notified by a woman who said she was his wife. They had married on April first (April fools day), and he was found dead on April tenth.

When I got the news, I felt frozen in time. I couldn't move or even show emotion. I felt nothing. It was an empty feeling, as if I should be sobbing or screaming or something. I felt like a stranger who called himself my father was dead, and all those times I cursed him for being so weak and hurting Mother and all of us over and over, not being the father he should have been or the provider he should have been or even a loving human being meant nothing anymore. He was gone, and I couldn't tell him how I felt or give him a chance to say he was sorry. It was meaningless.

The flight to Minneapolis was quiet. None of us spoke to each other the whole way there. I wondered, though, how my brother and sisters were feeling. They had Dad in their lives more than I. They knew him differently, and yet they weren't crying or showing emotion either. Was he hated by all of us, just for different reasons? When we stepped off the plane, there waiting at the gate was this heavy set woman in her late fifties with jet black and grey hair and dark circles around her eyes. She was very plain without any makeup and very animated, holding out her arms saying, "You must be Suzy, the baby." I just looked at her and wanted to turn and run back on the plane and go home. This woman was my father's new bride. She was more like the bride of Frankenstein. Out of nowhere, I began to cry. I can't really figure it out, but I just started to sob. My siblings looked at me like I was crazy and asked me what was wrong, but I just had to let it out. At the sight of this woman who claimed to be married to my dead father, I broke down. It wasn't because my father had just died. In retrospect, I was saddened by the loss of a father that I had never had. There had never been a real male role model in my life who showed me what it means to be a loving, responsible man. Only the strength of a woman, my mother who pulled her weight and provided for us children the best she could without any help or child support. My father was buried in a raw pine box in a paupers grave. There were only a handful of people at the gravesite, and again, no one spoke the whole way home. My father had a small insurance policy, which provided all of us kids with ten thousand dollars each. We thought we were rich. I moved into my own apartment and bought a new car. I was still working for the advertising agency and still doing a lot of partying. That money went fast. Supporting a cocaine habit is expensive!

I was on a road of destruction and eventually would crash. It took about six months of habitual using when I finally ran out of money and had to come to the realization that this lifestyle was either going to kill me or land me in jail. The advertising agency was starting to have problems. It seemed that one of the partners was skimming off the top and stashing away money for a quick escape to Mexico. Before this came about, I went crawling back home to mom again. It took a couple months to clean up, and coming down off of cocaine was not fun. My moods were up and down, and all that was left of what my father had left was my car. My mother saved my ass again and never made me feel like a loser. She was there with open arms and a shoulder on which to cry.

One night I was with a friend at a bar called Copperfields having a drink when I noticed a man sitting at a table alone. There was no place to sit, and I walked over to his table and politely asked if my friend and myself could join him. He was in his early forties or late thirties with thick black hair and a stocky build. He had a wonderful sense of humor and a pleasant voice. He offered us a drink and said he was waiting for his daughter to return from the bathroom. They were on their way to the Camen Islands and about to go to the airport. We talked for a long time until it was time for him and his daughter to leave. He said that his name was Ed, and he was a builder up in the north Georgia mountains and invited us to a Thanksgiving party at his place. I got his phone number and directions on how to get up to his home. He lived in the only ski resort in Georgia, on the border of North Carolina and Georgia. It was a ski resort during the winter months and a golf resort during the summer months. I was dating someone at the time who was taking off during that week on a fishing trip. It so happened that the week of Thanksgiving was also my birthday. Born on Thanksgiving, November 25, always meant a party along with a Thanksgiving feast. This time I was angry with the guy I was dating, and my friend couldn't go with me to the party, so I ventured up the mountain by myself. It was dark and the road was winding up the mountain. It took about three hours from where I lived, and I had worked that day, so I was tired. Once up the mountain, I entered a guard gate, which was the entrance to the resort. Somehow I found the house sitting on a hill overlooking the golf course and the waterfalls. It was so beautiful up there. The leaves had changed colors, and air was so clean and fresh. As I knocked on the door, I was greeted by a young boy with jet black hair and blue eyes. He introduced himself as Ed's son and to come in and make myself at home. His father was asleep, but he would wake him. The party was going to be the next day, and preparations were on the kitchen bar. The house had a smell of old cedar and the aroma of fixings for the feast we were to have the next day. They were expecting over one hundred people to arrive for the party. Ed awoke and saw me standing in the living room. He walked over to me and gave me a big hug and kiss. It felt like I had known him forever. Even though he was nineteen years older than myself, I felt at home in his arms. The setting was perfect, and he led me into the bedroom where he made love to me all night long.

Ed was a custom home builder who had lost his wife a few years prior from a surgery gone bad. He had settled with his three children up in the mountains where they could start fresh and he could give them a good education at a private school at the bottom of the mountain. His children where Will, sixteen years old; Kathy, fourteen years old; and Derrick, eleven years old. I was only twenty-one at the time, and this would be my twenty-second birthday.

The next morning came, and Ed had been up cooking for hours before I awoke. There was lots of activity, and I got to meet all of his children. Guests were starting to arrive, and there wasn't much time to talk about the night before. There were no feelings of awkwardness or being uncomfortable. It was as if I had found a place where I fit in, and everyone made me feel warm and wanted.

The trip was wonderful, and the party lasted through to the next morning. There were bodies of people who had passed out on the floor, and I stepped over them as Ed walked me to my car. He said he would call me, and I would be seeing him very soon.

He wasn't kidding when he said I would see him soon. The following day he called and said he wanted to see me. Within three months of seeing Ed and making several trips to the mountains, we discussed me coming to live with him. He said I wouldn't have to work and that he wanted me with him. It felt like a dream. I was swept away by the thought of living up in a resort and being taken care of indefinitely. Ed was not only my soulmate, but he was that father figure that I never had, someone who would love me unconditionally and give me the life of which I had always dreamed. All that glitters is not gold, however. There was a drawback. Ed was an alcoholic. He drank morning, noon, and night. He could still function and work. He built the most beautiful custom homes and had a good reputation as a builder. I thought I could change him. The first rule in life is never think you can change anybody. Life doesn't work that way. People only change if they want to change. I was young and wanted this relationship to work. Six months went by, and I met all of Ed's family. He met my mother and loved her like his own. We had discussed marriage and were planning a wedding in July. My mother was going all out, and we arranged to have a non-denominational female pastor marry us at the Marriott hotel in Atlanta. We would have our honeymoon in Las Vegas, which was Ed's favorite place in the whole world. The wedding was just beautiful, and we had a sit down dinner for about fifty people. We had the honeymoon suite at the hotel and had a party with an open bar and plenty of food. It was a good time had by all. Then it was off to Las Vegas the following morning, hang over and all. We had a blast in Las Vegas. Ed enjoyed playing cards at night while I slept and did sight seeing during the day. At one point, Ed was sitting at the tables and I was sitting at the bar drinking when a group of men entered the bar. One of the men saw me sitting alone and walked over to me. He put his room key on the bar in front of me and said he would meet up in the room in fifteen minutes. I was frozen stiff. There was a moment of silence, then I looked up at him and explained that I was not for sale and he was mistaken. I told him that my husband was at the tables. He apologized and walked away. I was blown away. Yes, he thought I was a hooker, and the thought excited me. I always fantasized about playing that part, and now the opportunity presented itself. I actually thought about it in that moment of silence and snapped back to reality. There I was, a newlywed and thinking about selling myself to a stranger. Crazy thinking!

When the honeymoon was over and we were back up in the mountains, everything seemed to go along well for a while. Ed wanted to give me the moon, no matter what the cost. He had bought a lot way up on a mountain behind the main lodge in the resort. We built a home on the side of the mountain, and Ed worked very hard all summer and fall. It was too cold to work construction in the winter months, so he had to make as much money as possible to get us through the slow times. Christmas was always important to Ed, and he was always very generous man during that time of year, mostly on credit and a lot of which was mine.

You see I started building up my credit at sixteen when I got my first credit card at the department store in which I worked as a clerk. So by the time I was twenty-two, my credit was excellent. Ed's mother was a wonderful little lady in her seventies when Ed and I married. She lived up in the north Georgia mountains on the border of Tennessee. Ed's father had passed away and left a house with several acres of land and two barns along with a small house for the caretaker. There was a pond in front of the house in which the kids loved to swim and fish. The house was very large with a full basement and screened in porch. It sat on the top of a hill with the view of the Blue Ridge Mountains, and the sunsets were magnificent. The farm was loved by all who visited, and Ed's mother, being a Southern woman, always had a feast waiting for us with fresh vegetables from her garden and baked goods made from scratch. The holidays were shared between his family and mine. We would spend Thanksgiving with my family since it was my birthday, and

Christmas was up at the farm with Ed's family, which worked out perfect since my family is Jewish. There was always a fire going in the fireplace, and the smell of burning wood and whatever was cooking at the time was so comforting. I loved it up there, and I loved Ed's mom almost as much as I loved my own.

The first Christmas at the farm is one that I will never forget. Derrick, Ed's youngest son, was in the back seat of our Camaro. It was a rainy night, and we were coming down a windy road almost to the turn off to Ed's mothers farm when one of the tires hit the edge of the road and Ed lost control. He screamed, "Duck!" and I put my head between my legs only to feel the car flip over upside down and slide. I felt mud coming at my face and legs as the car finally came to a stop. I thought for sure I was going to die. I was upside down and started yelling for Ed and Derrick. Ed's voice came first and said, "I am alright."

But I didn't hear Derrick's voice. I struggled to open the door and roll out of the car onto a muddy road. It was so cold and so wet. I couldn't see very far ahead or behind us. Ed rolled out of the car on his side. The roof of the car was completely smashed in, and the back window was out. There was no sign of Derrick, only gifts spread all over the road. I screamed Derrick's name over and over, and all of sudden, about fifty yards down the road, came a strange woman's voice saying, "Here he is." I turned to look, and, lo and behold, there was Derrick limping towards Ed and I with the assistance of this woman who had stopped to help. It was a miracle any of us had lived through this accident. The paper had a picture of the car at the accident, and underneath the picture read, "It was a holiday miracle that these three people walked away from this accident." Derrick walked away with only scratches and a sore leg after being thrown fifty feet out the back window. I look back at things like this and know that we do have a purpose, and there are guardian angels looking over us until our purpose here on earth is done.

After a couple years of living up in the mountains and having the freedom to ride horses during the day and party at the lodge at night, life got a little crazy. I was always meeting new people from different places. Remember, I lived in a resort. Ed spent a lot of time at the bar, and there were many nights I fixed supper for us, and I would call down to the lodge to find him at the bar when he was supposed to be home hours ago. Supper after supper was ruined, and I was alone most of the time. We were running up quite a balance at the lodge with dinners for perspective clients and friends of Ed's who lived in the resort year round that he felt a need to entertain on a regular basis. I stayed out of his financial business, and he preferred it that way. The oldest children were now moved out, and Derrick was in and out at will. I always got along very well with Ed's children except for his oldest son, Will. Will had a hard time accepting me and rightfully so. He was closer to my age than his father was. He tolerated me, and I did the same with him.

One night at the lodge, I was waiting for Ed to meet me after he got off the job. I sat at the bar and felt someone's eyes on me. I looked up, and across the bar sat a man with steel blue eyes, a cowboy hat, and the most beautiful, sexy smile I had ever seen. He started to walk around the bar towards me, and I could see that he was tall and was in perfect proportion with a double breasted western shirt and tight blue jeans. He wore a western belt with a large gold and silver belt buckle. He was dangerously attractive and had almost a evil look about him when he smiled at you, as if you weren't sure what kind of thoughts were going through this man's head, and did you want to know what they were, if you know what I mean. He came very close to me and asked my name. He said his name was Kenneth, and he was from Rome, Georgia. He was there at the resort to help a friend do some construction work. We talked for a long time, and when Ed arrived at the bar, he introduced himself to Ed as well. Kenneth was on my mind constantly after that. We would run into each other at the lodge, and always sparks would fly. He had told us that he was married to a dark-haired, dark-eyed Susan like me, but she would be staying in Rome with her mother while he was doing this job. Kenneth was close to Ed's age, early forties now, and I was turning twenty-five. Kenneth and I finally met away from the resort. We began meeting regularly at the top of a grassy knoll called "Thomas Knob." The afternoons were spent in the back of Kenneth's Blazer making love for hours. I knew this was wrong, but Kenneth was like an addiction, and I had to be with him. I didn't go into my marriage with Ed thinking that I would be unfaithful. I just was so lonely, and Kenneth was there. He was not just up at the resort doing a construction job with a friend, but Kenneth had a business on the side. He was a major cocaine dealer, and once again I began using. He always had plenty of cocaine, and as long as I didn't give Ed a hard time about his drinking, he didn't give me a hard time about my drug use.

Ed and Kenneth became friends, and my affair with Kenneth continued. Ed didn't suspect anything, and I couldn't stay away from Kenneth. I would even sneak out after Ed passed out from being at the bar and meet Kenneth in one of Ed's empty spec houses. Still, this went on for a couple years, then Kenneth's wife decided to move up to the mountains, and they got a hideaway where only a four wheel drive vehicle could go. There was a little cabin in the woods where Kenneth could go after a trip to the big city wheeling and dealing, then hide up in the mountains. At this time Ed, Kenneth, his wife, Susan, and I were spending time together. Kenneth and I had to cool things for a while, and Ed was losing his ass in the building business. The interest rates went sky high, and people stopped building second homes. The spec homes we did have were just sitting empty, and the construction loans were killing us. We didn't know how much longer we could hang on.

It was about this time when I received some devastating news.

My oldest sister, who lived in Atlanta with her two teenage sons, got diagnosed with breast cancer. She was to go in for a mastectomy and a biopsy, which would show if the cancer was benign or malignant. My mother, who lived in Atlanta still working as a bookkeeper for the Atlanta Jewish community center, was at my sister's side through the surgery. The answer came back as malignant, and my sister would have to go through a series of chemotherapy and radiation to see if they could slow the cancer down. Amy was only thirty-eight years old when she was diagnosed. She was a psychologist with a very successful practice. She raised her boys single-handedly and lived in a beautiful home near the governor's mansion in Atlanta. She was the sister who was fifteen years older than myself and never liked me. Now, she was dying, and family became important to her.

Ed and my sister had a bond and talked for hours sometimes. She would make visits to the resort and stay with us and take long walks in the mountains. Life took on a different perspective for her, and I finally got to know my sister for the person that she was on the inside. Her hair was gone, and she wore a wig or a turban. She was so pale and getting thinner as time went on. The treatments became so hard on her, and she became very weak. Amy had a friend who's family was very wealthy. They had heard of how sick my sister was and wanted to know if there was any place in the whole world that she wanted to go or see. Amy had always wanted to go to England, so tickets were provided by this family for my sister and her two sons to go to England as soon as possible.

The trip to London was not all that they had hoped. Not long after arriving in England, Amy became extremely ill. The cancer had attacked her liver, and she had to cut her trip overseas short and come back to the states. The boys were so scared. They knew that this might mean the end for their mother. Amy was taken straight to the medical center, and there she lay in a hospital bed with family at her side. I got to the hospital as soon as I could. When I arrived and walked into my sister's room, I was shocked. There was what was once a vibrant, beautiful woman, thin and drawn with the tint of gold to her skin from the jaundice. She had oxygen going in her nose, and she was so frail. There was this sadness in her eyes as she watched me walk to the side of her bed, and she held out her hand for mine. I put my hand in hers, and I squeezed. She had no strength to squeeze back. She said in her weakened whisper of a voice, "I am so scared that I will never make it out of here."

I was stunned. I didn't know quite how to respond. She was reaching out to her little sister for courage and a word of comfort. I looked at her and said, "I promise you will get out of here." I left the room with tears in my eyes, wondering if I would ever see my sister alive again.

I knew my mother was staying at my sister's house with the boys when she wasn't at the hospital with my sister. I, however, had to get back up the mountain and home, but would come back in a couple of days. As I was driving, I kept reliving that moment in the hospital when my sister took my hand. How could I have made that promise to her? She was going to die, and she knew it was soon. I spoke without thinking. I wanted to tell her what she wanted to hear. How could I do that? This would haunt me for the rest of my life. I would never make another promise I can't keep.

The whole time I was driving up the mountain to the house, I had this strange feeling, like I shouldn't be leaving Atlanta. Once I got home, Ed was waiting with open arms, and I fell in bed, exhausted. The phone call came at about three a.m. Ed picked up the phone, and it was my mother. He gave the phone to me, and I heard her voice shake as she said, "She's gone." There was silence on the phone, and I began to cry. I said I knew I shouldn't have left, and my mother assured me that no one could have known that she would die that night. Amy just gave up the fight and made her way to heaven on a September morning. I told Mother that I was on my way, and Ed and I left for Atlanta to be with the family. We all needed to be together at this time. Again, life would never be the same.

The funeral was long and sad with so many people I didn't even know. My sister had touched a lot of lives, and I never knew her well enough to know that side of her. She and I were like strangers for so long. My mother was sobbing and so was my grandmother. Her two boys were quiet with tears running down their faces. My sister was buried under a tall pine tree at a beautiful cemetery in Dunwoody, Georgia. My mother bought the plot right next to her, where she wished to be laid to rest.

Months went by, and Mother moved in officially with the boys. I had gotten my real-estate license and started marketing my sister's house. Cary, the oldest boy, was going off to a University in Washington D.C., and Craig, the youngest son, was to graduate high school and set off on his own. The house sold quickly, and Mother moved into an apartment of her own.

I continued to hang in there up in the mountains with Ed, but our financial situation got to the point where we were looking at moving to the city. Ed was a genius when it came to looking good on paper. He could come up with a financial statement that showed his building business as a multi-million dollar corporation. Things were very strained in our marriage, and his drinking had become a problem for me. Even with my drug use, I couldn't tolerate his continual drinking binges and his extravagant spending.

We sold our house in the mountains to a friend and business partner of Ed's and found a farm outside of Athens, Georgia in a town called Jefferson. It was forty-four acres with a barn, pool riding ring, a stocked pond sitting behind a 3500 square foot, two story house. It was so beautiful. Ed thought, if we could find a way to buy this property, we could live on the front acreage and develop the back wooded acreage. I was twenty-seven by this time, and I had told Ed that I wanted to start a family, that my biological clock was ticking. Ed had also gotten involved with a restaurant that had been for sale in Athens called Cattlemans Steak House. Ed wanted to run the restaurant and eventually be sole owner but didn't have the capital. Ed was a salesman from way back, and he somehow talked the owner of Cattlemans into selling him the restaurant on a contractual basis.

Yes, we did it. Somehow, Ed was able to borrow the down payment for the farm from his mother and Kenneth. Yeah, can you believe Kenneth and Susan were still in the picture and socialized with us on an occasional basis. I guess Kenneth figured, since he had been having an affair with Ed's wife for the past few years, he could at least lend him the money for the farm. Drug money or not, it was still a loan.

I thought I was in heaven. I put the life we had at the resort behind me and started to enjoy the place of my dreams. I had horses, dogs, cats, and ducks, and I was loving being secluded in this beautiful place. I could fish right off my back deck coming off the kitchen and feed the ducks by hand. I would wake up to mist over the pond and the sound of the whippoorwill in the distance. It was too good to be true. The only thing missing in my life was a baby. I knew Ed had a vasectomy and was willing to have it reversed in order to give me a child. He went to a urologist, and surgery was in the works. Unfortunately the surgery was a failure, and his sperm count was not enough to get anyone pregnant. The next option was invirtro. We went and saw a fertility expert and were given a list of sperm donors out of a sperm bank in California. After much discussion and reviewing the list of donors, we decided to go through with invirtro fertilization.

All I wanted was to be a parent and to stay clean for my baby. Ed, however, was playing the "I'm sober" game and would come home with the smell of mint on his breath, so I knew he was lying when he professed that he hadn't been drinking. I wanted this to work, and I was willing to completely change my ways of being wild and reckless.

The selection was made for the sperm donor, and now I was to take my temperature several times during the month. When it became elevated, I would drive into Atlanta and get artificially inseminated. The doctor said that in the ten years he had been doing this procedure, this was the first time that a patient got pregnant on the first try. I was with child and was so excited. I did not know if it was going to be a girl or a boy, but I felt great. I glowed and gained about forty pounds. Eight months into the pregnancy, I was making frequent trips to the doctor in Atlanta to check and make sure I was doing well. Meanwhile, Ed was making a go of the restaurant, and again I was spending a lot of my time alone. Finally, after two weeks of false contractions, I awoke from a dead sleep and felt something wet between my legs. Yep, my water had broken, and it was off to the hospital, which was three hours away.

My doctor was supposed to meet us there, so we were off to Atlanta. Once settled in labor and delivery, the doctor checked me, and I was not even dilated three centimeters. He had me walk around the hospital to hopefully move things along, but that didn't even work. He then started me on an I.V. drip to start inducing labor. This went on for hours. I was hooked up to all kinds of machines, and they were checking my blood count every hour to see if my white cell count was going up. Sure enough, my blood count was beginning to show signs of trouble, and my baby's heart rate was starting to increase. The doctor said he would have to take the baby since I never got past six centimeters.

They prepped me for surgery, and all I could see were bright lights as they wheeled me into the operating room. I could hear Ed's voice, and I felt nothing from the waste down. I heard voices everywhere around me, then the doctor began to cut. I felt pressure as he put his whole arm inside my stomach and pulled out the most beautiful baby girl. She was perfect. I heard the cry, and Ed got to hold her. He leaned her down to my face, and I kissed her cheek, then the room went to black. The next thing I knew, I was waking up in the recovery room. It was the happiest day of my life. My whole family gathered in and out, and they would bring my baby girl to me from the nursery every few hours to let her nurse from me. She weighed seven pounds even, and we named her Danielle Whitney.

We brought her home to the farm, and life would now never be the same. My mother spent a couple weeks with me and helped out. Ed was running the restaurant, and we didn't see much of him. The baby had her nights and days mixed up and was wanting to nurse all night and sleep most of the day. I felt like I was going out of my mind. She never seemed to get enough to eat from my breast and cried all the time. The only way I could get her to stop crying sometimes was to go for a ride in the car or keep her rocking in the battery operated swing. Her pediatrician diagnosed her with colic, and it just so happened that *New Parent Magazine* was doing an issue on colic in babies, and would we like to be in the issue? We agreed, and they came to the farm and took pictures and interviewed us. The article was named "The Baby That Wouldn't Stop Crying." Luckily, Danielle grew out of the colic stage, and I quit breast feeding her because it was driving me crazy. I thought I was going to be one of those mothers with postpartum depression who throws her infant off a bridge.

After mother left the farm to let me fend for myself as a new parent, I found myself very much alone again. My horseback riding days were over for a while until I could find someone to watch Danielle, and Ed was never around. I would take Danielle to the restaurant just to have something to do. Ed's drinking started getting much worse now, and there were times when he would have to stay in town and pass out in the restaurant, leaving Danielle and I alone. Ed's son still lived on the property, and that was the only thing that made me feel somewhat safe.

During this time, I would make trips into Atlanta and stay at Mother's just to have some company and help with the baby. This one weekend I was at Mother's, and Ed was visiting a friend on the other side of Atlanta working on some business when I received a call from Ed's son. All I heard on the other end of the phone was, "The farm is on fire." I stood there in disbelief. It was quiet for a second or two, then I began to scream, "Oh my God! My house is on fire!" Ed's son then said the volunteer fire department are fighting it now, but it was a total loss. I got off the phone and called Ed, and I could hear the slur in his voice and knew he was trashed. I was hysterical and crying but finally got it across to him that our home had gone up in smoke. He told me to meet him at the farm in the morning and that there was nothing I could do now. It was late and cold out and very dark. All I could think about was if the dogs were all right and how I could possibly get any sleep.

The morning finally came, and it was raining out, but as I drove down the long driveway to the farm, I could see the smoke bellowing from what once was my home. There were hot cinders everywhere, and all you could see was a black hole. Ed was already there with the insurance appraiser. I had left Danielle with Mother because I was in no condition to take care of her. I was crying so hard. I just walked around in a daze, taking a stick and trying to see if there was anything I could salvage in the ashes. My whole life had just gone up in smoke: my clothes, all my memorabilia such as my baby pictures, my wedding album, my ribbons and awards from all those years of showing horses, all of Danielle's baby pictures and baby book. I kept replaying all these irreplaceable things in my mind.

Again, life would never be the same after living through this. I kept wondering how this fire had even started. The investigators claimed it was an electrical short. I, however, had my own ideas of how it started. It was too much of a coincidence that both Ed and I were out of town when the fire occurred. Also Ed owed a lot of money to a lot of people, including a man who put the road in on the back seventeen acres. He was never paid and ended up putting a lien on the property. There were too many people out to get Ed for all the times he screwed them over, and I still, to this day, believe that the fire was no accident.

The days to come were very tough. I was staying in Atlanta with Mother, and Danielle was with me while Ed stayed in Athens camping out at the restaurant. We received our insurance settlement for the farm, and it covered everything and allowed us to buy a mobile home to put on the property until we could rebuild. I would help out at the restaurant when I could. On this one particular night when I was waiting tables, a tall, dark, and handsome man came into the restaurant. He had a salt and pepper mustache and wore a hat. He had these piercing eyes that looked right through you. It was lust at first sight. He began flirting with me, and I knew that life would never be the same.

We started meeting during the day, and with Ed's heavy drinking, I could depend on him staying at the restaurant most nights. My new love's name was Thomas, but he went by his middle name, Phil. He had been married before and had a young son about five years old. He also had a daughter with a woman with whom he had very little to do with. He was charming and incredible in bed. Little did I know that the next five years of my life would be a living hell.

He began by making me trust him and everything he said. He could see that I was done with Ed and the drinking. I knew he was going to bottom out soon, and I couldn't take anymore. I delivered his things to him at the restaurant one day and said it was me and Danielle or the bottle. His answer was, "I will not be given an ultimatum." I then handed him his things and filed for divorce. Our ten year relationship was coming to an end. Ed moved in with his son and later lost the restaurant. He moved to Atlanta to work with a friend on a construction project. He and I stayed friends and in contact at all times. Phil was insanely jealous of Ed and would do anything he could to hurt Ed behind my back. He would call his relatives on the police force and tell them to watch out for Ed drinking and driving. So, of course, Ed would get stopped. Another time Phil cut up Ed's convertible top to his MG. Phil was evil, but I had so much more to go through before I realized how evil he really was. Phil moved into the mobile home, and the farm was put up for sale. The money was going to be mostly mine to reestablish myself somewhere that was affordable. I had no skills and couldn't get a job living out in the country. Phil would pretend to go to work either painting or truck driving because he had his commercial driving license. The strange thing was, at the end of each week, he would never have a paycheck for one ridiculous reason or another.

One day I came home, and the trailer had been broken into. My jewelry was gone and the TV along with the VCR. I called the police, and they filled out a report. Later I found out through the investigator that the window was broken from the inside of the home. Which meant that it was an inside job, and guess who it was. Yep, my boyfriend, Phil. He had pawned the jewelry and various other things. I went absolutely crazy on him, threw him out, and demanded my jewelry back. He brought me to the pawn shop at which I paid to get my jewelry back. The other stuff was gone. Phil, however, begged me to take him back and brought me flowers, cried, faked a heart attack, did the whole thing, including promising it would never happen again. Stupid me, I took him back.

This was not going to be the last time he pulled the fake burglary routine. Just wait!

After a few months, things only got worse. We would have horrible fights in front of Danielle. She was only two and couldn't understand what was going on. Phil would accuse me of seeing other people and would constantly play mind games. He would take money out of my wallet and try to convince me that I spent it. Right when I was going to end it, I found out I was pregnant. I was in shock. What was I going to do? I couldn't stand the thought of having this man's child whose favorite names for me were cunt and whore. I called Ed, with whom I still kept in close contact. No matter what happened or how much I hurt Ed, he was always my best friend and would forgive me when I couldn't even forgive myself. He was very much against abortion, and my mother, who hated Phil, wanted me to end the pregnancy. I was so confused. I chose to keep the baby and try again with Phil. Crazy, huh?

Ed and my divorce was final, and Phil and I were still on the farm. The farm finally sold, and I found this rental closer to Atlanta. It was a mobile home on several acres of pasture for the horses, and the dogs would be safely fenced in. There was a barn with a loft that was from the slavery days. I thought this would be perfect, and the money from the sale of the farm could take us through until the baby was born. What a mistake this was. I stored all my belongings in the tack room right outside the home. Things there quickly began to happen that really can't be explained. As you would walk to the barn, there were areas of the pasture that were warm, then turned cold quickly. When you would step into the barn, you would automatically look up at the rafters and feel a sense of doom. Objects that were on the top of the refrigerator or on the counter would all of a sudden fall off. The dogs were one by one disappearing. I wanted to get the hell out of this haunted farm. I was seven and a half months pregnant, and I found a house in town that I could buy without qualifying and put down ten thousand dollars to get in. This was the plan after the baby was born. That night, I discovered the tack room had been broken into, and everything was gone. Here we go again. Guess who? Yep, it was Phil again. This time, a huge fight erupted, and all hell broke loose.

Phil had a rifle in his hand, and we struggled to the ground.

Danielle was with my mother, thank God. I saw the phone come flying at me. Phil was enraged, and every time I would get up, he would push me down. He would not let me leave. I felt myself going into labor. I screamed, "I'm going into labor, let me go." He let me leave, and I drove myself to the hospital. Once I got to the emergency room, they took me to labor and delivery. Phil was right behind me. I told them not to let him in. The contractions were ten minutes apart. The doctor put me into a birthing room and left me there for hours. Soon the contractions were only minutes apart, but my water wouldn't break. The doctor came in and said I could go home until my water broke. I yelled at him that, if he didn't break my water, I would have this baby somewhere else, and he wouldn't see a dime of my money. That changed his mind really quickly. He then stuck a plastic hard stick up inside me, and I felt the warm rush of blood and water come down my leg. Within one hour, I was completely dilated and ready to push. By this time, I was medicated and couldn't feel anything from the waist down. The doctor let me tear as I pushed my baby girl's shoulders out. At this point, Phil was outside the room, begging to come in and hold his new daughter. I gave in. After all this, I surrendered to his request.

The baby and I had to stay in the hospital for a few days because, due to the doctor letting me tear, we had contracted a strep infection, and both of us had to be put on I.V. antibiotics. Phil would come and go. The hospital sent a social worker in to my room to talk to me about why a new mother would be so sad. I guess the nurses had noticed me crying and the bruises on my arms and wrists. I just turned my head and said I would deal with my own problems. But the question was when. How long was this abuse going to continue.

We sold the horses and moved to the new house. I had this delusion that things were going to be different now—a new start and fresh beginning with our new baby—but things only got worse. I had no skills and could only find clerical jobs. Phil would go from job to job again, rationalizing why each job was wrong for him. He would call my job ten times daily to check up on me or accuse me of having lunch with one of the guys who happened to work there. Fights were almost daily. I never knew what would set him off. One day I was just lying in bed when he came in and accused me of playing around behind his back. He had a soda can in his hand, and he poured it all over me. He then spit on me and called me a slut. He picked up our daughter, who was only nine months old, and said, "Your mother was a whore when I met her, and she will always be a whore." The police were called on several occasions, but unless I was bleeding or the bruises were apparently new, they would do nothing except tell one of us to leave and cool off for a while. On New Year's night, Phil had been drinking, and we fought. He then forced me to have sex with him, at which point I fled the house. I slept in a battered women's shelter that night.

I would sneak off to battered women's meetings because everyone who was close to me was staying away because of Phil. I had nowhere else to turn. He would tell me that no one else would want an overweight, single mother of two children from different men except him. I was so sad and so lost. I felt like my identity had been taken away, and little by little I was crumbling into nothingness. It wasn't long before I found myself pregnant again. This time I went to a counselor for abortion options. Little did I know that the place were I went was a pro-life office and showed me films that would turn your stomach. I began to weep and left, knowing again that I couldn't go through with an abortion. I wanted a boy so badly. All my adult life, I wanted that boy who I could go watch play little league and who would have my heart. I just felt like this pregnancy could be that boy I had always wanted. Sure enough, the ultra-sound showed the baby being a boy. I was overjoyed. Even with Phil in my life, I was so excited. There was one problem: I had what they call placenta privia. The placenta was below the baby, which could be dangerous, and the baby could be premature if I was not careful.

Month after month went by, and Phil and I somehow were surviving the fights. He would say he was going out to get a paper and not return for hours. It was always lies. He then asked me to marry him before the baby was born. I was only thinking of the baby when I said I would. I didn't want to have another baby out of wedlock. Silly me.

I really don't know what I was thinking because, deep in my heart, I knew Phil and I were like oil and water, and we were destined to fail. We had a small ceremony with a non-denominational pastor who was a friend of my sister's. We wrote our own vows, and at the end of the wedding, my mother came up to Phil and said, "If you ever hurt my daughter, I will spend the rest of my life making you pay." Phil knew she was serious. Time went by, and things seemed to be going well for a few months. I was out of school and working as a cashier at a local grocery store, standing on my feet for hours at a time. Meanwhile, I never knew what Phil was up to or if he was going to bring home a paycheck from week to week. The doctors warned me that standing on my feet was not the smartest thing to do in the last trimester of my pregnancy. Knowing I had placenta privia and could begin to bleed at any time, I should have been taking it easy. Somebody had to make a living, however. I was six weeks early, and I began to bleed. The doctor said to come into the hospital and an emergency c-section would be performed. I was scared, and it was late in the evening. Danielle and Courtney, my daughters, were so small, and someone had to watch them. My mother could not come, so they came to the hospital and lay down with their pillows and blankets in the waiting area. I remember some neonatal specialist asking me if I was taking any drugs, which I wasn't, and that she would take care of the baby when it was born. They quickly took me into surgery, and Taylor Garrett was born five pounds fourteen ounces. They said he was anemic and needing to stay in the hospital for a couple days to be monitored. Other than that, he was perfect. I was so happy to have a little boy. My brother sent me the most beautiful roses, and everyone came to see my son. Danielle and Courtney loved their baby brother and enjoyed helping with his care. Phil was a proud papa and was very good with the baby.

Time passed, and financially things became more stressful and more difficult. I placed Taylor and the girls in daycare as soon as I could get back to work. Daycare centers, as you know, are nothing but sick pits where the kids pick up every illness imaginable. We were about to lose the house because we couldn't make the payments, and again the fighting was starting. We put the house on the market right away, and within a month we had a buyer. We could get enough money out of the house to relocate, and I could go back to school. We ended up buying a double wide mobile home in a community park with other small children. It had a park and church on the premises along with activities for the kids. It was a clean, well-kept environment and had a community pool. I applied for grants and enrolled in the nursing program at the community college. There was a program for displaced housewives that really helped me with uniforms and books. I was studying three and four hours a night while also taking care of the kids. Phil was painting here and there and would help with the kids at times. It was hard, but I had to stay focused on what I needed to do in order to support my family. Sometimes the fights would escalate, and the neighbors would call the police. The kids would be crying, and Phil would have to leave, but he would always be back, telling these babies that their mother was a slut and accusing me of having affairs at the college. There were times I felt so unbelievably alone and wanted to end my life, and then I would take a look at my children and get back to what I needed to do. I knew the end was in sight, and my pity party had to go away.

You want to know what's really funny? At this time, I responded to a talk show called the "The Beatrice Berry Show," and the show was going to be about spousal abuse. The show flew Phil and I out to Chicago, and a big black limo picked us up at the airport and took us to a hotel downtown. It was located near the studio where we would go out in front of the whole world and make total fools out of ourselves. I used to say, "Where do they find these people?" Well, here we were. Phil had no idea what was to come when we stepped out on the stage. I cried and discussed the verbal abuse as well as the bruises and pop cans being spilled over my face and head, the lies and the constant disappearance of items that he pawned for money he supposedly made that week. The audience crucified him. He looked like such a fool when it was all over that I was scared to return to the hotel after the show. He was surprisingly calm and collected, almost like it hadn't bothered him at all. My family had taped the show, and to this day, I cringe at the thought that I lived through this hell and survived.

Then some wonderful things started to happen. My English teacher in college helped me compose a letter to several different scholarship programs. The letter won me three scholarships that year. One of the scholarships was being presented in St. Petersburg, Florida, and they flew me out there, and it was one of the best times of my life. I stayed in a hotel with almost five hundred other women who had come from all over the US to participate in this award ceremony. It was awesome. I received over five thousand dollars in scholarships to keep me in school and assist in living expenses. At this time, Phil and I had enormous fights again, and I had to get a restraining order against him for domestic violence. I had no idea what I was going to do now. Alone, in school, and not knowing how I was going to make ends meet, I went and got food stamps, and this was around Christmas time. I had no idea how the kids would get Christmas.

I called a friend named Glory who headed a women's Bible class at Hebron Baptist Church in Ducula, Georgia. She took me to her class one day, and there were about sixty women in the room. People I just met were handing me checks to continue in school, and the church paid my bills for a few months until I graduated. Not only that, they also did Christmas that year. My children had twenty presents each under the tree. When they asked me what I wanted, I told them they gave me my Christmas already. Still, there were twelve gifts for me under the tree. They provided Christmas dinner and a box full of goodies for me and the kids. I had never experienced so much unconditional love from people in my life. I will never forget those wonderful people, true Christians. I began going to this church, and I loved it. They had great programs for the kids, and daycare was provided. I felt at home. Glory was my angel that year. Angels come in different shapes and forms, but they are all around us, and I will talk more about that later in this book. I lost touch with Glory, but she will have a place in my heart always.

It was spring, and Phil and I were off and on for a couple months. He would always return like a bad penny and beg my forgiveness. The kids would be yelling, "Daddy" and lifting their little arms for him to pick them up. I would violate the restraining order over and over again. It was time for me to graduate, to walk the line and take my nursing vows. My whole family was there and my children, and, yes, Phil was there, too. I was in line, wearing my white nursing dress and shoes. It was time to be capped and pinned by my instructors. As I was walking down the isle to accept my diploma and cap and pin, I flashed back on a time in my youth. I was on a bus going to the beach, and a lady was sitting in front of me. She turned around and just looked at me. I asked what she was staring at, and she said she pictured me in white. I was used to all the California nuts, but she said she was a psychic and saw me in a white dress. I asked if that meant a bride, and she said no, a nurse.

I never gave it a second thought because, at the time, I was only fourteen and had never thought of wanting to be a nurse. Now, here I was. In only a matter of seconds, I would become a licensed practical nurse. Tears filled my mother's and my sister's eyes as they called out my name. We celebrated afterwards, and from that moment on, I knew life would never be the same.

Phil moved back in with us, and I had to search for a job. I was hired instantly at a nursing facility close to home as a staffing coordinator. I would do all the new hire physicals and immunizations along with doing a med pass when nurses would call off or be on vacation. I started there at $11.50 an hour. I wanted to get out of the mobile home park because of the embarrassment from all the police calls, the shouting, and the yelling and to start somewhere else. We sold the mobile home and rented a house in a nearby neighborhood. The rent was $800.00 a month, and I wasn't sure if we could manage it, but with this new job, I thought I would try.

Within two months of working, Phil and I were at it again. Only this time, it was really ugly. He was causing problems at my job and would leave for days at a time on road trips, but he still never helped pay anything. He had his CDL and would jump from one trucking company to another. I was at the end of my rope. I knew that, if I did not leave the state, I would end up either killing him, or he would kill me. I started planning my escape. I had filed for a divorce and with the help of my family I got that taken care of. Phil was supposed to give me $400.00 a month for the two kids and all the health insurance. Ha ha. This never happened.

I always wanted to go back out west, and now was my chance. I had $3,200.00 saved up, and I needed to decide where I wanted to go. It was a choice between Arizona and Colorado. I knew that I couldn't afford to go back to California, so I ended up choosing Arizona. I had my aunt and uncle there along with some old friends from school days in California. An old boyfriend and his sister and her family invited me and the kids to stay with them until I got a job and on my feet. I had it all planned to leave when Phil was on one of his so-called road trips and then take off. Ed was going to drive the U-Haul across country, and I would drive behind him. I hated the thought of leaving my family, but they knew I had to go. The day before we were to leave, it was snowing outside. The ice was forming on the roads, and the gas had been turned off in the house, and all we had was a wood stove to keep us warm. I had gone to the wood pile and purchased as much wood as my small car could hold and opened the stove, which was electric, thank God. We all cuddled up together, me, three kids, and a dog and cat. The morning came, and it was sleeting outside. In the cold and sleet, everyone pitched in and loaded up the u-haul and car, and we wept as we said our goodbyes to Mom and my brother and sister. I had never in my whole life lived in another state then my family. This was a very sad and scary moment. Life would never be the same.

When Phil came back and found us gone, he flipped out and said I would never see a dime from him since I took his kids out of state. I did notify him through a certified letter, letting him know how to get in touch with us and in what state we would be. No address was given, however, and I knew he was too much of a redneck to ever leave the South. We would finally be free of him and safe.

We made the trip in four days, did about five hundred miles a day, and stayed the night in hotels along the way. Somehow, we finally made it to Arizona and to my friends' house, Jack and Stacy. Jack was a year or two older, but he was my first sexual experience. My best friend in school, Andrea, was always in love with Jack, and now we were all grown up. Andrea was happily married with two boys, and I was there with Jack. Crazy, how things turned out. Stacy, Jack's sister, had three kids and was also happily married. All of us were staying at Stacy's house until Jack's new house closed, and then we would all move in there. At least that's how it ended up. Jack and I hooked up and became a couple almost immediately. Because I was moving into his new house with him, I agreed to use some of my savings to help with the down payment. The understanding was that, if the relationship did not work out, I would get back that money and move out.

It came the day to move into the new house. I had gotten a night position at a nursing facility once my license was transferred from Georgia. Jack was with the kids at night while I worked, and he worked during the day. The kids were in elementary school, and I would see them off in the morning and awaken when they got home. We only heard from Phil twice, and then he stopped trying to contact us. He even tried to tell the nursing board that I was on drugs to punish me for taking the kids and leaving. The nursing board made me take a witnessed drug screen to clear myself from these charges. The courts could never find Phil for all the back child support, and quite frankly, I was just so glad he was out of our lives.

Life with Jack wasn't all it was supposed to be. We would argue about food and that there wasn't enough for him and the rest of us. He would complain about the kids touching his stuff and messing with his big screen TV. He drank a lot of alcohol, which affected his performance in the bedroom. I had lived with an alcoholic, and I didn't want to do it again. When I told him how unhappy I was, he offered to marry me, but that was not the answer. The answer was to move out and stand on my own two feet and get on with my life. I could tell that I hurt him terribly, but I had to do it my way. He paid me back the money in increments, and unfortunately it got ugly at the end. I had to sue him for my money. I continued to be friends with his sister, which was a really big mistake.

With Stacy's help, I moved into a two bedroom apartment near her house and ended up putting a lot of stuff in storage. Ed was back and forth from Las Vegas, where he was living, and helped me with this move. Once again, he came to my rescue. Somehow he was always there for me and the kids when we needed him. My son and I had one bedroom, and the two girls shared the other bedroom. It was crowded, but we managed.

Ed stayed with the kids at night, and I worked my night shift at the Nursing Home. I was fairly new at the nursing thing, and I was in charge of a whole unit with thirty-two patients. The other nurses would meet outside on break and smoke. Yes, I picked up the filthy habit, too. There was an English woman who worked for the lab that the facility used, and she would come in every night to draw the patients' blood, and we became friends. Her name was Trish, and she was my only friend in Arizona. We would go out on Friday nights and drink and meet guys. We would dance and get crazy on my weekends off. Ed used to call us the two teenagers. One night at the bar, we met these two guys. They were identical twins and very handsome. Both had sandy hair and were thin, with beautiful blue eyes. One worked for a computer company, and the other one was a radiology tech. They were fun, and I hooked up with the radiology tech named Kevin. He and I talked all night, and he happened to be living with his parents at the time, so he started coming over regularly. Ed really liked him and so did the kids. He would call me "beautiful." I thought I had met the man with whom I would spend the rest of my life. He was the best lover and wanted nothing more than to please me. He cleaned the house and started staying the night. Ed went back to Las Vegas for a while, and Kevin moved in with us. He was supposed to be watching the kids while I was at work. One night I got a call at work that the kids were alone. Kevin decided to take a walk to the bar near the apartments while the kids where asleep and put down a few beers. When I got ahold of him, he denied leaving and then said he was only gone briefly. A big red flag started waving in front of my eyes. This was the first time I felt like he couldn't be trusted but certainly not the last.

I had been doing very well at my job and had excellent credit. I thought it was time to see if I could buy a house. I met with a realtor and found this lovely tri-level in a great family community with a park and community pool. It was ninety-two thousand dollars, and I was making thirty thousand dollars a year. The news came that I was approved, and I bought the house with my tax return as my down payment. The payments would be 785.00 dollars a month. I was so excited. We would be in an 1800 square foot house with four bedrooms and fruit trees. I never thought I would ever get this far after what I had been through.

Once settled in the house, everything was good for a while. Kevin moved into the house with us, and he turned into a mad man. He started yelling at the kids to clean up and was always fighting with my oldest daughter, Danielle. It became a daily struggle with him and the kids. He wasn't working and was just hanging out at home watching TV. I would come home, and the kids would demand my attention and Kevin would get angry and start yelling. He would cause scenes in public when it would be just he and I. If another guy so much as spoke to me or looked my way, Kevin would confront him and it would be so embarrassing. He once threw my daughter's CD player down the stairs in a fit of rage. If we were in a restaurant and the kids did something he didn't like or approve of, he would cause a scene. Once he disarmed my car because he did not want me to leave the house. It was like a nightmare happening daily. What happened to that wonderful human being I thought was, my one and only? I had gotten a day shift at a facility not far from home, and Kevin had Taylor in his truck. Apparently Kevin had been drinking and decided he would take Taylor to my job and do donuts in the front yard of the facility. My supervisor, not knowing who he was, called the police, and Kevin was taken to jail for DUI and child endangerment. I was standing outside watching this take place.

Finally, I told Kevin I had enough of this and wanted him to leave. It took a restraining order and the police to get him off my property. I felt like I was reliving Phil and my relationships in so many ways. How do I keep getting involved with these psychos? I knew it was a cycle, and I wanted to break it. I began going to battered women's meeting and finding out that I was not alone. There were lots of women living a life like mine and suffering with every unhealthy relationship in which they found themselves. They all said the same thing: when you first meet these men, they seem so wonderful. They are usually really good lovers and manipulators. They come off as being perfectly normal and suck you in, and then they show their real selves.

There was a lot of learning I needed to go through to find out why I kept making the same mistake over and over again. I saw that red flag, and instead of being drawn to it and thinking I could change or fix people, I ran the other way. The only person who could fix me was me, and being a natural caregiver and nurse, I was more apt to be a magnet to those who need me much more than I need them. Just when I thought Kevin was out of my life, he showed up on my back porch, dowsed in gasoline, threatening to set himself on fire if I didn't take him back. The police were called, and Kevin was stripped naked in front of my house and hosed off by the fire department. I thought I was going to die. The neighbors got out their lounge chairs and popcorn and watched the show. Kevin was then taken to a behavior unit at the hospital. He didn't' stay long. He ended up going to jail and losing his radiology license; all of which he blames me for. I have also learned that these people take no responsibility for their behavior or the consequences from their behavior.

Now I was alone again, but for the better. I could now focus on my job and my kids and get a better perspective on how life needed to be. It was a slow process, but I reached out for help and used every resource out there to learn about me as a person and to respect who I was and be true to myself. To depend only on me for all that I wanted in life and not depend on others to make me happy or complete. I started to feel a personal power, a sense of growth and hope. I had people in my battered women's group who were still struggling in an abusive relationship, and I wanted to help them find freedom and a new strength and self esteem. Abusers make you feel like you are worthless to everyone but them, that they are the only ones who can love you and will take on your kids. I was told over and over by Phil that I was fat, and just look at me. He would say, "Who would want you and your kids except me?" It was all about control and power. Well, I had taken back the control and the power, and with support and encouragement, I would never let it happen to me again.

I had to be strong and be a role model for my children. I had to show them that I would not tolerate someone beating me down and pushing me around. I wanted them to know what a healthy, loving, give and take relationship can be like, or the cycle would continue, and they, too, would find themselves where I have been. We have to overcome for the sake of our future generations. I wanted my children to be proud of their mother and know that no matter what happened in the past, the future would take precedence and hopefully make those horrible memories of abuse fade away.

Unfortunately, my oldest daughter lived through the brunt of the abuse, which I could tell took its toll on her. She became very angry and unable to respect any man who would come into my life. She had a issue with trust, which was very legitimate after all that she had witnessed as a small child. Now, as she was entering her teenage years, I could see trouble ahead. She was a very intuitive child, and her respect for me as her parent and role model had been tarnished with all the times I allowed myself to be violated. Yes, I allowed these things in the past to happen to me. Now I had to fix it somehow and help my children heal.

It was a cold day in November and Ed had been living up in the north Georgia mountains at his mother's farm, caring for her. She had Alzheimer's and needed to be taken care of until she could be placed into a nursing facility. Ed hated it up there, and his drinking increased considerably. Once his mother was placed, he had to stay and watch the farm and try to sell it. He was so alone up there and would call Danielle periodically just to talk to his daughter. He was supposed to come to Arizona and spend Christmas with us. Meanwhile, I had been approached several times at my job by a hospice agency that was trying to recruit me. The hospice nurses would come in and check on the patients who were on hospice care but still seen in the facility. They had tried to get me to come and join their agency for over a year when I finally agreed to try it for six months. This is what they suggested as a period when you see whether hospice is for you or not. I was to be part of the team that goes into the nursing homes where the hospice patients reside and assess them. This was an arena where I was comfortable, and I was very excited about this change in perspective in nursing.

The first few months with hospice were very difficult. I wasn't sure if this death and dying thing was something I could emotionally handle. I had seen people die in the nursing home setting but not in great numbers. I watched and learned from the other nurses and would witness the compassion and love they would show to their patients. We would see patients in the home setting as well, and then it was a different ball game entirely. You were on their turf, and sometimes it wasn't pleasant. You would walk into fighting families or older adult children living off the terminally ill parent or stealing the patient's drugs. You dealt with angry spouses and filthy living conditions. Sometimes, however, you became one of the family, and they would look forward to your visits.

My first patient I lost in the home setting was a little old man from Chicago with lung cancer. He had never smoked but had worked in the mills and had lung cancer from asbestos. I had a difficult time with this situation because I wanted to be there when he died, but I wasn't. Another nurse was on call that night. I felt like I had in someway abandoned him and discussed this in a debriefing meeting they have for new hires. Now I knew what they meant by giving it six months to find out if this fits for you. Things got better as I realized that I worked with a team and was not just me out there. We, as a team of professionals, worked together, the social worker, the pastoral counselor, the aide, and the nurse. We had each other to depend on, and I needed those people for support to care for the patient. I started questioning my own life and death. I became more appreciative of every day God gave me. Instead of feeling sad, I fell in love with hospice and brought joy and laughter to families and patients. I could make the rest of the days that they had left more dignified and comfortable. I had a gift, and I found it through hospice. The traveling around doing visits was putting a lot of wear and tear on my van, so I opted to take a position in one of the units. We had several ten bed facilities where Hospice patients would come for crisis reasons. Some would come in to give the families a respite, or others would come in to die. Whatever the case, this was going to be what I was to do for years to come.

It was my day off and early in the morning when the phone rang. It was Derrick, Ed's youngest son calling from Georgia. "It's Ed, isn't it?" I asked.

"Yes," he said. Ed was found at the farm in a pool of blood and was non-responsive. He had gone into acute liver failure, and a neighbor found him. She had to break the glass to get into the house. Now he was at the Blue Ridge Hospital and only had hours or days to live. He was on several machines and was in a coma. Ed's family was there along with his daughter, Kathy, and oldest son, Will. I was shaking and crying listening to Derrick. He asked if we were going to come, and I told him I would call him back as soon as I told Danielle. Danielle was just awakening to go to school when I called her upstairs. We sat on the stairs together as I told her about her father. There was a long pause of silence. I saw tears building in her eyes. I knew her head had to be flooded with thoughts of her father. I asked her if she wanted to go and be with her father.

She looked at me and said we couldn't afford to go, so just send a message to school when he died. I responded by saying we couldn't afford not to go. I told her she was not going to school, and we would find a way to be with her father. I then called the nurse taking care of Ed and explained that we were coming and to tell Ed to wait for us. I knew from my hospice training that the hearing is the last sense to go, and he would wait. She assured me that she would tell him. I told Derrick we were on our way.

I had a friend whose brother happened to work for America West airlines and offered us buddy passes to get to Georgia. We got the passes and packed our bags. My girlfriend would watch Courtney and Taylor while Danielle and I would fly to Georgia. Once in Atlanta, it would be another three hour drive to Blue Ridge. It was dark and rainy when we finally arrived. Exhausted from the mountainous roads and the flight, we walked into that little hospital and down those horrible odorous halls to a small room. Danielle and I entered the room and immediately saw Kathy at the bedside. She jumped up to hug us, and we all cried. I looked over at the bed, and Ed was lying there with a glowing tint of orange from jaundice. He had a suction tube coming out of his nose that was removing the blood building up in his belly. His eyelids were wide open, and his eyeballs were moving from side to side as if he was in a constant seizure. He had an I.V. through which they would administer medication and a catheter for his urine, which was a bloody tea color. Danielle just looked down at her father and cried. I asked several questions about his care and could see that he would not have wanted all these tubes in him. It was fine in order to give us the time to get there, but now that we were the last to come, I would take control and demand that the tubes be discontinued. I told Kathy and Danielle to go back to the farm, and I would stay at the hospital with Ed. Danielle and Kathy kissed Ed and said goodbye, then drove about twenty miles to the farm where Derrick was waiting.

This was my time to say goodbye to my soulmate. Ed had always been there for me and loved me unconditionally. He put up with all the pain and shit I had put him through along with the relationships and the moving. I told him I loved him, and I would see him again. He would always have a part of my heart, and his love for me was what got me through so much. I knew how much he loved the kids, and they knew how much he loved them. He was the only one they all called, "Daddy." I told him that it was okay to go to that beautiful place and let go whenever he was ready. I told the nurses that I wanted the suction tube disconnected, and, although she agreed to do it, I ended up doing it. The nurse came in and said, "Who took out the tube?" and I looked at her and told her I was a licensed nurse in Georgia and I took it out. She walked out and said not a word. I sat by Ed's side and noticed he was beginning to twitch. The shaking became increasingly dramatic, and I called in the nurse. Ed was having a seizure and needed to be medicated immediately.

Once the seizure was over, I explained to the nurse that Ed was an alcoholic and needed to be medicated appropriately or he would seize to death. She was ignorant to such additional needs and, with lots of prompting, finally called the doctor for better orders. That was still not enough. Hours went by, and the doctor would make rounds in the morning. I got maybe one hour of sleep. Ed had two seizures through the night, and I couldn't wait to talk to the doctor. The sun was coming up and Derrick showed up at the hospital. The doctor finally came in and he was some foreign physician who was rude and had no bedside manner. I was very stern with him and the nurse about Ed's imminent condition and end of life care. They wanted him out of the hospital before he died. They actually were talking about the kids taking him home to the farm and caring for him until he died. I could not believe the stupidity of these people. Here Ed was hours away from death and I had to fight to get him meds and let these people know that he was not going to be moved. I just wanted him to be comfortable and not seize to death. Medicate him appropriately, is what I said over and over. We walked back into Ed's room after this horrible meeting was over, and I went to wipe the jaundice liquid from Ed's eyes when I noticed Ed was starting to seize again. This time it was a big one, and I yelled to Derrick to get the doctor. I opened the window to let the soul fly free, which I often do in hospice, and I told Ed to go. "Go now," I yelled to him. "You need to go now, Ed, no more suffering. I love you," and with that, he took his last breath. The doctor and Derrick ran into the room after the event, and the doctor pronounced Ed dead. The doctor looked at me, as the tears ran down my face, and said, "He's comfortable now." I replied, "Yeah, because he's dead." With that, I ran out of the room. I ran and I ran. I did not even feel the ground below me. I ran out the hospital doors and out past the parking lot. I came to the grass in the very front of the hospital, and I fell to the ground. I was hysterical, crying and looking up at the sky and yelling to God, "How could you let him die that way? Why, just make me understand why he had to die here, now, and this way."

In that instant I felt someone touch my shoulder. I looked up and there, bending over next to me, was a beautiful woman with reddish blonde hair and blue eyes like the sky. She had such a sweet, angelic voice as she said that she saw me running and fall to the ground. She felt like I needed her and that she would like to give me a hug and a prayer. I asked her where she had come from since I didn't hear her come up behind me, and she said she had just gotten off her shift at the hospital. We prayed together, and she held me for what seemed to be a long time, but in actuality, it was only moments. All the pain and anger was gone. Only sadness remained as she walked away and left. She said her name was Kathy. She was gone as fast as she had appeared. I slowly got up off the grass and walked back into the hospital. When I entered the hospital, I began questioning the staff as to who Kathy, the nurse, was. They all stated that there was no Kathy who worked there or who matched that description. I knew I had met my guardian angel. Who was that stranger? It was meant to be, and her face is engraved in my mind forever. I had the faith and the strength to go back to the room and call Danielle to let her know her dad had died.

The girls got to the hospital and sat on the bed for a while. Kathy held her father and rocked him in her arms, weeping while Danielle sat quietly with tears rolling from her eyes. I hugged her, and I knew she would miss her father terribly, even with the memories of him being drunk most of the time, the times as a little girl when she would be sitting outside waiting for her daddy to pick her up and him never showing. Even with all the bad memories, there were so many good ones. Ed always worshiped Danielle. He used to call her the center of his universe. She knew this and loved him so much. This was a really hard loss for us all, and life would never be the same. Christmas that year was very sad. Ed was supposed to be there with us. We made it through the holidays and the other, older kids had Ed's ashes, which would eventually make it back to us. He wanted his ashes spread over his favorite place, Laughlin Nevada. This would take a while to accomplish, but it would finally happen.

It was hard to concentrate at work. I thought a lot about Ed and our twenty-two years of friendship and ten years of marriage. Who would be there for me now? He was my rock and my biggest fan. I also needed to help Danielle get through this. She would never talk about her father or his death. Every time I would approach her with the subject, she would say there was nothing to talk about and that her dad was dead and just leave it at that. As a matter of fact, I was very worried about her. The other kids were also having some difficulty since they were so close to Ed and had several questions about death and heaven. I wanted my children to have faith that there is a heaven and there is something after we are done here on earth. "Death is a part of life," we will all reach that time eventually, and it is not something to fear is a hard concept for adults, much less children. I have reached this understanding only in recent years and have no fear of death, only the process of getting there.

As time went by, things got easier, and a new year was upon us. I was trying to still go out with Trish on a regular basis and would meet different guys and have one night stands periodically. I wanted no real relationships or commitments, just casual sex and fun. I wanted to enjoy being single, in my forties and still sexy. I was independent and working two jobs to support the household. I was working at Hospice during the week and doing agency work on my days off. I was exhausted, but it was so nice to come home to a family who loved you and a place you could call yours.

During this period of time, my youngest daughter, Courtney, was in a car with Stacy and her two girls. Remember, Stacy is Jack's sister who we lived with when we first moved to Arizona. Her family had moved to California and had come to town to visit. They were going to take Courtney with them so she could spend part of the summer with her girls. Stacy was driving, left Arizona at 3:00 A.M., she fell asleep at the wheel just before crossing the border into California. The girls were not wearing seat belts. The car flipped twice, and Courtney and one girl flew out of the back window. Stacy and her other daughter in the front were trapped in the car. I got the call at about ten that morning. I was at work, and a nurse from a hospital in Needles, California said my daughter had been in an accident. I felt my heart drop to my stomach, and I said "Is she alright?"

The voice on the other end said, "Yes, she will be alright. Would you like to talk to her?"

Courtney's little voice came on the phone and was crying, "Mommy, please come get me." I was crying and said I would be there as soon as possible. I left work and got in the van and drove for five hours until I reached Needles. There were no airports near there, and driving was my only option. I walked into the hospital and saw Courtney with bruises everywhere. She had a black eye, and her right arm was in a sling. They released her to me and said that they thought the elbow may be broken and to confirm with an orthopedic when I returned to Arizona. The one other girl who was thrown from the car was the least hurt, and Stacy and her daughter were flown to Las Vegas General Hospital for trauma injuries. It was a miracle that they all survived.

When we returned home, the doctor confirmed that her elbow was not just broken but crushed. It needed surgery and screws, and a rod would have to be placed. He was worried it would affect her growth plate, but the arm still would give her problems in her future. Stacy's insurance company only allowed Courtney so much in compensation, and then I had to go to my insurance agency for extra coverage. Courtney would have thousands of dollars in a CD when she turned eighteen from the accident. This doesn't make up for her elbow or even her life. I never spoke to Stacy after that and never want to again. I almost lost my child, and for those parents who dread that phone call, just praise God for every day you have your children.

When life started getting back to normal, I met this man at the bar to which Trish and I used to go. His name was Michael, and he was single with adult children who live out of state. He had that Kenny Rogers look with the gray beard and mustache. He was very easy to talk to, and we started making it a ritual to dance with each other every weekend. I invited him over to meet my children, which would usually end things really fast, but he didn't seem to mind the chaos at all. They got along fine. So, one night we were at the bar dancing, and Michael turned to me and asked if I wanted to go to Las Vegas for a few days. I looked at him like he was nuts and wondered if it would be possible to get time off and a babysitter in such short notice. I replied that I would love to go if I could make it happen. Well, I got busy and was able to produce not only a babysitter but I got another nurse to cover my shift. I was on my way to Vegas with Michael.

We arrived in Las Vegas after traveling for six hours and checked into our hotel. Michael was from Michigan, and a couple friends were flying into Vegas and meeting us the next day. That night was for us. On the way, Mike mentioned a conversation he had with his friends before leaving. They were all drinking beer and laughing and told Mike not to take off to Vegas and get married. He just looked at them and said, "Why not?"

They were all quiet, then responded by saying, "Well, we don't know why not." When Mike told me this and waited for a response from me, I just laughed it off and said that would be crazy.

We spent that first night in Vegas gambling and going to a comedy show. We were having a great time. When it was time to go to bed that night in the wee hours of the morning, we made love, and Mike turned to me and said, "Why don't we get married?"

I said, "You can't be serious." He was very serious. I attributed it to the alcohol, and we talked for hours about life, kids, and what he would be walking into if we were to get married. We both left it at that and would discuss it at daylight when we were both sober. Daylight came quickly, and Mike had gone to get coffee and brought it to me in bed. He then approached the subject of marriage again. This was madness. I hadn't known Mike that long, but somehow everything felt right. He was kind, fun, and worked hard as a mechanic. I tried to think of the negatives of marrying him and there were none. I was having a rough time with the kids turning into disruptive teenagers, and Taylor needed a male figure and discipline badly. I thought this could be a good thing for all of us. Yes, I thought I loved him, but not the way I had loved before. He was a friend, and I felt a closeness that could survive the test of time.

I agreed to the marriage, and we went out and got our license and found this cute little wedding chapel next to our hotel. It was a little white chapel with flowers everywhere, and it was so warm and inviting. And, no, Elvis did not come out and marry us. The pastor who married us had a European accent, and his wife was a witness. The ceremony was beautiful, and, with jeans on and no real wedding ring, Michael and I were married, and again, life would never be the same. Of course, the first person I told was my mother, my best friend. She was so delighted, and I had her promise not to tell the kids. I wanted to be the one to break the news. She said she would only tell my sister and brother. The rest of the trip was wonderful. We met up with Mike's friends and told them, and they celebrated with us. Mike bought me a beautiful band with diamonds at the jewelry shop in the Hilton, Las Vegas. The next day came, and I was to fly back home while Mike would stay and visit with his friends another day. I had to get back to work and home.

My friend picked me up at the airport and immediately congratulated me on my marriage. I was pissed off that she knew, which meant that the kids already knew. Yes, it was Mom. She couldn't wait to call home when I got off the phone with her and broke her promise. I asked how the kids where taking the news, and all my friend said was they couldn't wait to see me. Oh no. I walked into the house, and I yelled, "I'm home." I called a family meeting.

As Danielle was climbing the stairs, she said, "How could you get married without talking it over with us first?"

I knew I had work to do before Michael came back the next day. I discussed my feelings towards the marriage and tried to make them understand how wonderful life could be with a healthy, male figure around. Of course Taylor, only being nine years old, thought it was a great idea. Courtney, being twelve and already promiscuous made the comment, "We can get him out of here in six months," and Danielle, being fifteen, just said she didn't care, but I knew she was angry at me for the "quick mistake," as she put it. It was quite a meeting. I knew this would be a difficult transition and the kids were going to test Mike as much as humanly possible. He took it like a soldier when the girls started getting into legal trouble. Courtney and Danielle would get caught for shoplifting, or Courtney would take my van and go joy riding until one time she got caught by the police. It was the typical teenage nightmare. Still, Michael and I endured.

We sold the house that I had bought and bought a larger house with a pool and a place for Mike's RV, in which he had been living. The house was four bedrooms and a den with a beautiful fireplace. It was a home I had only imagined ever being able to buy. Mike and I gave it a shot, and we were approved for the house mortgage. We were so excited to have this fresh start together. The problems with the kids' behavior didn't end just because we moved. The girls started having friends over who were stealing from us. One kid wrote "Big Fat Jew" in black paint on our garage door because he was mad at my oldest daughter. Our marriage still withstood this hell we were living with the girls.

I was on the phone with my mother a lot during this time and asking for her advice. She always had a way of making a bad situation better. She did it with love and without judgment. I could hear her breathlessness as we spoke, and I knew her lung disease was starting to get the best of her. She was diagnosed with COPD, which is chronic obstructive pulmonary disease from smoking since she was eighteen. I got off the phone with my mom and called my sister, who lived close to my mother and would take her to all of her doctor appointments. I asked her about my mother's health, and she hit me with the news I had dreaded all my life. It seems back in January—and now it's April, mind you—the doctor told mother that she had maybe another year to live, that her disease had progressed and there was nothing left for him to do. My mother chose not to tell me at that time, and my sister and brother promised her that they would not tell me. I knew she was oxygen dependant, but I was left in the dark, and I was so upset. I told my sister that she had no right to keep that information from me. I could have moved back to Georgia and taken care of Mother. I never would have bought the new house. My sister told me that mother was so happy about the marriage and didn't want to spoil things for me by giving me this news. I said that should have been my choice, not theirs. I still could not get over being left out of the loop. I did not confront mother with my knowledge because I knew we were coming out to Georgia for her eightieth birthday in a few months, and we would talk then. I wanted Michael to meet my mother before something happened, and I knew it could be her last birthday on this earth.

It was August, and we all arrived at Atlanta airport, two adults and three children dragging their luggage through the huge crowds of people. Finally we got to my brother's house, where some of us where staying. The girls were going to stay at mom's apartment. We rushed over to see mother and walked into her little two-room high rise senior apartment to find her hooked up to her oxygen and pale as a ghost. Her breathing was labored, but she was sitting on the couch and gave us all her huge smile and hugs. We kissed her and sat around her, holding her hands and staying very close, as if just being in her presence made everyone happy and at peace. She had a way of doing that. We stayed with her most of the day and night and then went back to my brother's to get some rest. The party would be tomorrow, and everyone in the family would be there. We were all to meet at the Red Lobster for lunch, where we would open gifts, be together, and celebrate.

The next day came and we went over to Mother's. Mike and Mom got along great, and she really liked him. She called me into her room, and I sat on the end of the bed with her. She held my hand and said, "Now that you are happily married, I can go in peace." I began to cry because I knew it was her way of saying goodbye. She knew the end was near, and she always said eighty was old enough, as if she predicted her fate, and that was the magic number. She began giving away things of hers, like her jewelry and pictures. This trip was her closure, and I really didn't grasp it at the time. Lunch time came, and we had Mother in a wheel chair with her oxygen, and off we all went to the restaurant, my sister and her adult children, their children, my brother, and my nephew from LA. The other nephew still would have nothing to do with the family but was invited to the birthday. It was a joyous celebration, and yet through it all, I had this sick feeling in my stomach that I was losing my best friend in the whole world. When the party was over and we were all back at the apartment, I insisted on sleeping with my mom that night. I just wanted to smell her and hold her in my arms. I just listened to her breathing, so deeply and struggling with every breath. I felt the tears running down my cheek. I didn't want to leave my mother, and yet I knew my life was back in Arizona with my family. I had to trust that my sister and brother would look after Mother and meet her needs. I discussed hospice with everyone, including Mom, and they thought it was a good idea and would check into it that week. I only knew how wonderful my agency was, and I assumed all hospice agencies ran the same. It came time to end the trip, and we all cried as we said our goodbyes.

Once home and back to work, I would call mother daily to check on her. The hospice agency they chose provided medications, a visiting nurse, a social worker, and a pastoral counselor. I thought this was great until I began making calls to the agency to find out the status on my mother. No one would talk to me. They said that they could only give information to my brother and sister. I quickly got on the phone to my brother and sister and told them that they had better give me information about my mother. They promised this would change immediately, but when I made the next call, the nurse was very vague. She knew I was a hospice nurse and gave me attitude over the phone. I just wanted them to treat me like a concerned daughter and not their enemy. Most of the information I would get was from my brother or from Mom herself. I knew they started her on morphine for her breathing, but she began sounding confused on the phone. She was always groggy and would slur her words.

After a couple months of this, I began to really get worried. Being almost two thousand miles away and not really knowing what was going on was driving me crazy. I was calling my brother every few days and asked if Mom was eating and drinking. He said when he checked, a lot of the food he had bought her, was still in her freezer. All these horrible thoughts started running through my mind, like Mom didn't even have the breath to make a frozen microwave dinner. She needed more help, and I couldn't be there to help her. Something was wrong with this picture, and I was going to get to the bottom of this.

I began making phone calls to Hospice in Atlanta, and finally a very rude nurse, who was taking the place of my mother's regular nurse, spoke with me. She told me that my mother's nurse was on vacation and she was covering for her. She then said that, with her last visit, my mother's vital signs were all right, and she seemed to be okay. I said that when I talked to Mom last night, she sounded confused and groggy. She could barely breathe, and I was very worried about her care. The nurse on the phone was not concerned, and I knew as vague as she was, that she really didn't care. I got off the phone, and I was furious.

The next morning came, and I had to work that day, a twelve

hour shift at the unit. I barely slept that night and was worried about my mom. I called her apartment, and no one answered. I really was worried then, so I waited and called back, thinking maybe she was in the bathroom, but still no answer. I looked down at my cell phone, and there was a message on my voice mail. It was from my brother, saying that Mother had been taken into the hospice unit at the hospital for medication management but that she was okay. I quickly called him, and he explained that Mom was not managing her meds at home well, and she needed to be in the unit for a few days. He said that she was eating a McDonald's hamburger, one of her favorites, as they brought her in. I guess that was to make me feel better about this whole thing. Little did any of us know, but that McDonald's hamburger would be my mother's last meal.

As soon as I got off the phone with my brother, I called the unit where my mother was. The nurses, again, were very vague on the phone and would not let me speak with my mother. I called several times that day, and every time I would call, they would say that my mom was asleep. Being a nurse and dealing with this on a daily basis, I knew something was very wrong. As the day progressed, I could feel my mother calling me from two thousand miles away. I felt her pain, and whether it was mental telepathy or just the fact my mother and I are so bonded, I could hear her calling for me to come to her. I had a sinking feeling in my stomach as the panic began to fill my body.

There was a patient on my unit at the time whose son happened to be a very successful motivational speaker. He would travel all over the country doing seminars, and I knew he could help me with a ticket to Georgia really fast. I explained the situation to him, and he gave me the number of his secretary, who helped me. She took my credit card information and booked a flight out the next morning. I was never computer savvy and did not even own a computer to do all this on my own. I called my brother and told him about my travel plan, and he was completely okay with it and would pick me up at the airport. I really knew then that, if he was so receptive to me coming, that I was completely justified in the way I was feeling.

The plane ride was so long, and I couldn't wait to see my brother and find out how Mother was doing. I got off the plane, and there he was, waiting in the baggage area. We hugged, and he said Mother was doing okay from what the nurses told him earlier that morning, and we could have a bite to eat somewhere before going to the hospice unit. I agreed, thinking he really knew what was going on, but in retrospect, he didn't have a clue.

We walked into the medical center and went up an elevator. I started getting nervous, like something was very wrong. After walking past the nurses station, I entered a room that was old and had that hospital odor. I looked to my right, and there was my mother. You could hear the rattle from her lungs as I walked closer to the bed. She had a glazed over, distant look in her eyes. I had seen that look several times in my unit when patients were actively dying. I went to her and hugged and kissed her and told her I was there. I felt this horrible sinking feeling in my heart and became ill. I rushed out to the hallway and hit the wall as I went to my knees. I looked at my brother as the tears ran from my eyes and said, "How could you? Did you not know that our mother is dying?" The nurse down the hall came running when she saw I was on the floor. I was hysterical. My brother tried to comfort me and said he had no idea, that no one called him. I was sad, but most of all I was angry. How could this be happening? The nurse said she didn't know that no one was told, and that the doctor had just made rounds that morning.

I tried to pull it together; however, I was traumatized, and I told my brother that Mother was only hours from death and to call everyone. He quickly got on the phone and started calling my sister, nieces, and nephews, even my aunt and my cousins so they could say goodbye to Mom on the phone. I called the kids right away to talk to their grandma, and they were all weeping over the phone as they said their goodbyes. Remember, the hearing is the last sense to go, and there was so much to say with so little time. My mother looked so uncomfortable. She was restless, and she was like a fish out of water. Her lungs were full of fluid that she couldn't cough it out, and she was too weak to swallow. She had a foley catheter in her bladder that was draining bloody urine. She must have had a urinary track infection and no one bothered to notice. This happens quite often in the elderly when they are on opiates and are not drinking enough. It also causes confusion, which Mom had when I spoke to her last. Were these home nurses not doing their job, or did they just not care? I had to wonder.

I couldn't stand to see my mother in so much discomfort with that "death rattle getting louder." I called for the nurse who kept syringing morphine and ativan in my mother's mouth to calm her down and help with her respiratory distress. It would calm her only temporarily. I kept asking her if there was anything else she could give her, and the nurse brought in a huge syringe with Benadryl. My mother was choking because she couldn't swallow. I immediately told the nurse to stop. I asked her to call the doctor for better orders, and she stated that she had plenty of orders and she would not need to call the doctor. I was becoming ballistic. My brother assured me that it would be alright, but I knew Mother was struggling. She struggled so much in her life, why did she have to struggle in her death? Then that term we use in hospice now popped into my head, "We die the way we live." Please tell me that's not true. During the quiet moments when Mom would be calm and all you could hear was her breathing, I just sat next to her and held her hand and told her how much I loved her over and over again. I told her what a great mom she had been and that she would be missed, but we would be alright. That everyone was on their way and that I had heard her calling me two thousand miles away. "I will see you again, Mom," was what I told her. I was losing my mother, my best friend, my role model, the only person I could always go to no matter what. I couldn't imagine life without her. I was a family member now, not a nurse taking care of the dying patient, but I had to advocate for my mother. I stayed on that nurse to medicate my mother appropriately. It wasn't enough meds to let her die comfortably. I asked the nurse to try several things, and she would say that they did not do that in their hospice unit.

Everyone started showing up, one by one. Craig, my estranged nephew, who had not talked to mother in years, came into the room. My brother had even reached him. I couldn't believe my eyes. Everyone gave Craig time alone with mom to make his peace. I do not know what he said to her, and that is between them and God. Everyone gathered around Mother's bed, taking turns talking to her and saying their goodbyes. The crying could be heard outside the room. Mom's breathing was changing, and there was only one person left to come and that was my niece, Erica. I told Mom to hang on, and with that, Erica and her husband walked into the room. Erica ran to Mother's bedside and held her. I wanted to crawl in bed one more time with my mommy. I knew she was going.

She all of a sudden became agitated, and I ran out to get a nurse, frantic, saying, "You have to make her death peaceful, please do something." I ran back into the room, and my brother was at my mother's side with her cheek resting on his fist supporting her neck. She was breathing so quiet and shallow, what we call guppy breathing. You couldn't hear that rattle any longer. I opened the window for her soul to fly free, and she took a few last breaths and stopped. I screamed, "Mom!" and she looked startled and tried to take another breath but couldn't. I, unconsciously, kept her from the light. I did not want to see her go. My brother gave me that mean look of his, and I knew I shouldn't have been so selfish. She had flown away with everyone who she loved all around her. I wept and threw myself on the other bed in the room and pounded the mattress. I was devastated. I had only gotten off the plane six hours before my mother took her last breath. It wasn't long enough, and it was so unfair that no one knew, and she was all alone, unable to verbalize her pain. I will never get over how my mother died. I will have that vision of her when I first walked into that hospital room for the rest of my life. It haunts me even four years later.

We all then waited for the mortuary to come get mom's body. She was supposed to go to Emory University for research, but she still had the burial plot next to my sister. We nixed the Emory thing and had her cremated and her urn buried next to my sister. We then all went our separate ways. We were all exhausted and upset, and I went back to my nephew's house to spend time with him. After all, the last time we talked, he was a teenager, and now he was a man. We had a lot of catching up to do and things I needed to understand. We talked until three or four in the morning, and a lot of things got resolved for us both. I was so glad he could make peace with mom before it was too late. I felt like I was in a fog. This was just a really bad dream, and I would wake up soon, and everything would be as it was before Mom got so sick. I was walking around in a daze. Now I knew exactly how my family members felt after their loved ones died at my unit. I went back to my mother's apartment the next day and met my brother and my nieces over there to start getting rid of some of Mom's things. There were things the kids wanted of Mom's, and we needed to agree together. It was so hard to go through her things. I crawled into her bed and hugged her pillow, and I could smell my mommy, and the tears began to flow. I wasn't dealing with this whole thing very well.

My brother flew my two daughters in for the funeral, and my nephew, who was the closest grandson to my mother, came from Los Angeles. I picked the girls up at the airport, and everyone was so quiet as we proceeded to the cemetery. The home care nurse from hospice was there, the one who had been on vacation, and the pastoral counselor from hospice was also there. She was very close to my mom. She sang a song that my mother had liked when she would visit her in the home. Everyone was there, even an old friend of my sister Amy, next to whom Mother was being buried. I was shaking, standing above this hole in the ground where Mother's urn was to be placed. I had written something the night before and was trying to hold back the tears as I read it out loud to everyone. It was all so final, and my words came from the depth of my soul, so you could hear a pin drop as I spoke. Mom was my hero, she was our rock, she raised three children by herself, and we never needed for anything. She was where I got my strength, my survival instinct. For all that, that she had given me, most of all, her unconditional love and she was always my friend. I closed with part of a quote from my favorite children's book called "Love You Forever." I said, "I'll love you forever. I'll like you for always. As long as I'm living, your baby I'll be." Then I sat down and lost it.

My nephew, Cary, got up and talked about mom and made us all laugh talking about her love of jelly beans and circus nuts, and, oh yeah, don't forget that horrible candy corn. She loved all that sweet candy and would eat it until she was sick. He talked about fun stuff and happy memories, then the pastor sang, and we closed the service with a prayer, and my brother placed my mother's urn in the hole, and before any dirt could be placed over the urn, I requested everyone's attention. I looked at everyone and then looked up at the sky and said, "Okay, Mom, now you can smoke all you want," and I took a cigarette and put it in the hole with the urn. Everyone chuckled as they began walking to their cars. I knew, from that day forward, life would never be the same for any of us.

My nephew, Craig, had everyone at his house after the service for refreshments and had platters of food for everyone. It lasted about an hour, then we knew it was time to go back to mom's apartment and start packing. We were going to fly back the next day, and there were lots of loose ends to take care of. I gave the girls things I wanted them to have from Mom and a coin collection for Taylor. We all were cried out and exhausted. A lot of mother's things were donated to the apartment complex for others who might need them. That last night at Mother's was hard, but in a very comforting way. Danielle, Courtney, and I felt close to Mom by being there and had a night of "remember when" talks. We laughed and cried together and did the things that we all used to do on our visits to see her.

The trip home was quiet and sad. I couldn't let go of my anger at the way my mother died. It was wrong, and I, as a hospice professional, knew all about good deaths and bad ones. Mother's, as far as I was concerned, was a bad one. I got on the phone the next day after arriving home and called the supervisor with hospice in Atlanta. I needed some answers for my own peace of mind, and I was going to get them.

I spoke to a supervisor and stated all my concerns in a very angry tone of voice. She knew I was very upset. She said she would get back to me after reviewing the chart. I also requested that I get a call from the hospice physician who saw mom the morning I got in town, the day she died. She assured me that I would hear back from her and the physician.

The next day came, and I was going back to work. I was still grieving, and I had no idea that my agency offered bereavement paid time off. I could take a whole week off. I began my shift, and that afternoon I was called into the social worker's office by two supervisors. They sat me down and proceeded to lay into me about how I had spoken to a family member about my mother's situation, which was a breach in agency policy, and I was being written up for it. They questioned me about the ticket to Atlanta and how I acquired it, and did the family member pay for the ticket? I found out later that the family member had been called and questioned about this matter along with my co-workers, and they already knew the answers to these questions. I started to cry as they continued. They said, "Who do you think you are?" and asked me if I thought I was special, and didn't I have any computer savvy?

I informed them that I don't even own a computer, and I had to get to my mother no matter what it took. They told me that I had crossed the line and made me sign my write up. They were so cruel, I couldn't believe this was happening to me. They ended the meeting with, "You need to get bereavement counseling ." I walked back to the nurses station crying. How could the people I worked for be so insensitive? I felt like my spirit had been broken and a knife had just been dug into my heart, as if it wasn't already breaking. I could barely work the rest of the day. I kept thinking about why I didn't just tell them to go to hell and walk out of that office and never look back. I would never forget or forgive that meeting. They weren't going to break me or make me change who I was. I had to keep my priorities in order and work to support my family. I knew hospice was my gift, and they were not going to be the cause of leaving. If nothing else positive came from all this, it was that I was going to be an even better hospice nurse and advocate more for my patients, not to allow any of my patients to die the way my mother did. I took my five days of bereavement time off.

During the course of those days, I received a phone call from the hospice in Atlanta. It was a conference call with a group of staff, including the supervisor talking to me. I wanted to know why no one was notified in my family that my mother was actively dying? One member stated that it was documented in the nurse's notes that a family member was called. I replied that it was a lie, that no one received any such call, and I did not know what family was called, but it wasn't my brother or sister. I also asked why the nurse didn't call the doctor for better orders when I asked her to in order to make my mother more comfortable. They stated that it was an error on the nurse's part not to call the doctor, and she had been reprimanded. I began to cry. I asked why the doctor didn't document in his notes how bad my mother was and have the family called? They said he had written that my mother had "rales and wheezes" in her lungs that morning and did not write or say that she was actively dying. I told them that my mother had more course sounds in her lungs back in August when she turned eighty then that, and there was no way he could have written that. Then I really got upset and demanded that the doctor call me. I then asked how they could allow my mother to die like that and still call themselves "hospice providers"? There was silence on the phone, and then they all apologized, which didn't make things any better. I told them that I hoped to God they learned something from my mother's death and they wouldn't let others die like that. They replied that the bereavement department would be contacting me, and I firmly said, "Don't bother," and I hung up the phone. I knew I had gotten my point across. I then waited for the doctor to call me.

The next day came, the phone rang, and it was my mother's doctor. Finally, I could get this resolved. I heard his voice on the other end, and I began to shake as I started asking him questions. I asked why, if he had seen my mother that morning, he didn't have the family called and how he could write in his notes that she only had wheezes and rales when I knew better. He denied that he wrote that and did say her lungs were congested, but she did not appear to be close to death that morning. He had assumed the nurses were keeping the family informed on her change in condition. I then asked why the nurse would not call him for better orders that night. Was he out with his family and didn't want to be disturbed or what? He replied that she should have called, and he was sorry that she didn't under the circumstances, that he was accessible by pager. I then asked why was my mother so under-medicated. Did he not know that she had a long history of Valium, Ativan, Xanax, and other sedatives? I told him that, since I was thirteen, she had been taking these drugs. Did he not read her history and physical? There were a few seconds of silence, and he then replied he had not read her history and physical and had no idea about her long drug use. I started to cry and stated that I could not understand how he could appropriately take care of a patient without doing his homework. He again apologized, and I could not hold back and told him he should be ashamed of himself, and I then said this conversation was over and hung up.

He shouldn't have been allowed to be a hospice physician of any kind if this was how he took care of the dying. I was appalled, I had to get a grip on things. I was overwhelmed with grief and felt like my whole world was tumbling down around me. My brother and sister, who did not know any better, thought Mother's death was the way it was supposed to be, and my brother even sent the nurses flowers for taking care of Mom. I wouldn't let them know the way I was feeling or my conversations with the hospice staff at that time. They did not need to feel the way I did. Sometimes knowledge is a terrible thing. I would later tell them both everything.

Time passed, and things seemed to get a bit easier. I was visited once by one of our agency bereavement counselors, and she advised me to go to meetings with other adult children who had lost their parents. I declined and said I was not the kind of person for that. I had to deal with things my own way, and I did. The holidays after my mom's death were very somber. No one really was into the holiday mood, and we just wanted it to pass quickly. I wanted it to be a new year that would be better for us all. With time, the pain became less and less. I still find myself, four years later, crying out of the blue, calling out for my mother. I still beat myself up over not advocating more during her death. I believe I could have done better for her, but I was so traumatized. I had a feeling of doom that day but had no real thought that this would be the day that I would lose my mother forever.

I ask myself why all the time and still look for those little signs that tell me that she is doing all right up in heaven, whether it be a rainbow or a butterfly that passes by, or a dove flying in front of my van out of nowhere, any sign, that brings me peace of mind. When I see a daisy, my mother's favorite flower, I smile and think of the bunches of daisies I used to get her on her birthday and Mother's Day. I miss her so, and I just want her back is what I always end up saying at the end of the day, even though I know her body is gone, and in spirit, she will live forever. I look in the mirror, and I see her. I see her eyes and all the features passed down from her. I know she is inside me till the day I take my last breath.

Time passed quickly, and life was getting a little easier. Mike was very supportive during this time, and his mother had been ill recently. She had to undergo abdominal surgery for masses they had found. When they did the surgery, they said that she could not have any more, and what they found was cancer. She was terminal, and we did not know how long she would have. During the next year, she slowly became weaker and weaker until a hospice in Indiana got involved, and Mike's brother and sister were handling her affairs. Up to this point, she had been very independent and active. She was a wonderful woman with a heart of gold very much like my mother. Mike and his mother were very close, and he knew he would have to make a trip to see her before too long. His brother and sister kept us informed. Now he needed my support, and I would be there for him like he was there when my mother was dying. Mike made that trip and saw his mom while she was still alert and he could talk to her and laugh with her. She was taken to a hospice unit near Mike's brother's residence, and there she could get the end of life care she needed. I stayed in the background and knew my place was at home, and Mike, like me, had to handle things in his own way. He came home very sad but knowing the trip was so valuable to him and his mom.

We were out that night at our favorite watering hole when Mike got the call. It was his brother and sister. His mother had just passed away. It was almost one year to the day when my mother had died. It was very eerie. They said it was very peaceful, and Mike knew he would have to make another trip for the funeral. He drove all the way back and brought back a lot of his mother's things with him. His adult children had been with him, and he got to spend some real quality time with them. I offered him a lot of love and support and knew the next few months would be tough. I was still grieving over the loss of my mother and now this. Any more deaths in this family would probably put me right over the edge.

During this time, we were having difficulties with the kids. The girls were not getting along with Mike very well, and my oldest daughter, who had bared the brunt of my earlier abusive relationships, had lost two of the most important people in her life, her father and her grandma. I wanted to help her, but she just shut me out. Being a mother of teenagers who have gone through so much wasn't going to be an easy job. I had to be the one to make it better. I needed to fix it, and I wasn't sure how. Mike and I were working hard at our marriage and trying to work and make ends meet. Our paychecks were spent before we even got them. I knew we were no different than most American families, but it still put a strain on the relationship, and, therefore, the kids were affected. Again, time tends to fix things on its own. With much love and understanding, we were able to endure, the financial difficulties and arguments about the kids. Our disagreements were few and far between, and I never had to worry about Mike hurting me or hurting the kids. He treated me with respect and never called me names or struck me. He didn't lie or cheat or steal. I was going to work hard to make my marriage work as long as he felt the same way and was equally as committed. We could communicate and resolve any issues together.

Things were settling down, and the kids and Mike were actually starting to adjust and get along. He was working hard as a mechanic, and I continued at the hospice unit Danielle, my oldest, was graduating high school, and I was a very proud parent. My nephew from Los Angeles came out for the ceremony. No one else from the family could get away to attend. She was a little disappointed about that, but we had a big party afterwards for her friends and the family. It turned out fine, and I knew this was another big step for my daughter towards adulthood. She didn't know what she was going to do, so she decided to work for a year and figure it out. No problem, and I told her she could live at home as long as she wanted. There would never come a time when I would throw one of my children out on the streets. She and I had never been really close, but I had always loved her with all my heart and soul and reached out to her the best way I could. I remember how hard it was trying to figure life out at her age, and if she needed some time, I wasn't going to pressure her.

My career as a hospice nurse has been a real adventure, and I have to share some stories that might actually make a believer out of you. I know they did me. We have this interesting call light system in our hospice house. The nurse's aide holds a pager, and when a patient pushes a button at the side of the bed, the pager will go off. That is how we know that the patient needs assistance. Well, I had a patient the day before who had died in room seven. The room had been cleaned and was empty, ready for another patient to come. The aide and myself were standing in the kitchen, and it was very still and quiet that day. There was no wind outside. All of a sudden, the front door flew open and a gust of wind came into the unit. Almost instantly the pager went off. We looked down at the room number it showed, and it was room seven. I looked at her, and she looked at me, and we ran to room seven. The button was not pushed in. I yelled out, "Florence, you can go now, there is nothing here for you, and it is time to go home to heaven." We then walked out of the room, shut the front door, and there has been no sign of Florence since.

Another time when we were bathing a patient who was actively dying, we experienced what I would call a "spiritual happening." The family had been at the bedside for hours, and this patient did not look imminent, so we took the opportunity to ask the family to step out of the room while we freshened him up. They obliged us, and we began the bath. His name was Jim, and we had the window cracked while we continued his cares. There were pictures on the bulletin board next to the window that were of his family, and it was very quiet outside, again, no wind. All of a sudden, a gust of wind came in through the crack in the window, blowing off all the pictures on the board. I looked down at Jim, and he was gone. The angels had swept in and taken him right before our very eyes. I cannot explain the feeling we had when that wind came rushing all around us. It came in and just as quickly left, taking him with it. I had to explain to the family, and thank God they understood. We let them in, and they stayed at the bedside for a while, then left. I was so incredibly in awe at what I had just experienced in that room. The aide felt the same way.

We have these memories of life and death experiences forever. We have to believe that there are angels and they are all around us in different shapes and forms, even those we cannot see. I know, I do believe because I have seen and felt them. I continue my work in hospice because I get back so much from the families and people for whom I care for. They all touch me in one way or another. I hear their life stories and their regrets along with the good memories while they tell me their life review. I learn so much from them and take a little bit of knowledge and wisdom with all that they offer. Who says it's just about what I can do for them? The hugs and kisses, holding a patient or family member while he or she weeps, making sure that my patients die with dignity and comfort, that is what I give to them all, unconditionally, and expect nothing in return. And yet they will never know how much they give back to me. Many families come back to the unit just to see me again because I made such a difference in their lives, as a person, as a nurse, and as one who truly cares. I have no regrets in choosing this field of nursing and cannot imagine myself doing anything else.

I was nominated for the compassionate care award and have a Certificate of Hospice Excellence on my wall. I have much of which to be proud. From a beaten down, not wanting to live, state of mind, to now. What a difference. I have come so far. My oldest daughter, Danielle, starts her first year of college this fall. My youngest daughter, Courtney, wants to pursue a nursing career like her mother. My son, Taylor, is in Junior High and wants to play football professionally. I told him he can accomplish anything he wants in this life but to always have a back-up plan and get a good education. He agreed. Life is a day to day struggle, but we accept whatever comes our way. We have lots of animals running around our home and enough love for them all. I am very blessed to be here, now knowing where I have been.

I have been hit, kicked, pushed, bruised, and I have had cans of soda spilled all over my head. I have been spit on in front of my children, which, to me, is the ultimate insult. It's like saying that I'm not worth the ground I walk on, not to mention the names I have been called that no one should tolerate. I can only say that I have been there and will never allow myself to be there again. My two younger children have not heard from their dad in several years. He owes me hundreds of thousands of dollars in back child support, and you know what, I don't care. My children and myself are safe and much better off without him in our lives. You have to be safe and be respected, not just for yourself, but for the future generations who think it's okay for Daddy to hurt Mommy. Save the children! It is not okay, and you have to break the cycle of abuse before your children and their children perpetuate this atrocity.

I am worthy of being happy, I am worthy of being safe, and I am worthy of being truly loved and respected. Keep saying this to yourself over and over until it sinks in. I am special, and so are you. No one can abuse you without your permission. Take the next step and reach out for help. There is a ton of assistance out there for you and your children. All you have to do is want it badly enough. There are people who will teach you a trade or assist you with going to school. There is daycare assistance and restraining orders along with legal assistance to keep you and your children safe. Yes, it's scary at first, but don't give up. Use the system to better yourself and to become strong and self- sufficient. That's what it's there for. And when you're feeling like this is all too scary and you could possibly continue in the relationship, beware, that is where you have to stop and think about the future and use your resources, call someone who can remind you what hell on earth is really like. Look at me and know it can be done, and it will all be worth it in the end.

This book was ten years in the making. It's been a long journey with a lot of wild ups and downs. There were times I did not want to relive the things that have happened in my life and could not bring myself to remember them. We have to face our fears and take chances to better our lives. Isn't that what we have all been put on this earth for? Always be true to yourself, and all will work out for the best. We all have two things in common, we are all born, and we will all die. Make this adventure count, have more good memories than regrets, and tell the people in your life that you love them every day because you never know when it will be your last.